Jesuits, Theology, and the American Catholic Church

Daniel Kendall, SJ, and
Gerald O'Collins, SJ

Paulist Press
New York / Mahwah, NJ

Cover images: background by Shane E. Davis / Shutterstock.com; top left, Georgetown University, by Orhan Cam / Shutterstock.com; top right, St. Mary's Hall, Boston College, by Jerry Coli / Dreamstime.com; bottom courtesy of Marquette University; Society of Jesus logo by mojahata/Shutterstock.com
Cover design by Sharyn Banks
Book design by Lynn Else

Library of Congress Cataloging-in-Publication Data
Names: Kendall, Daniel, author. | O'Collins, Gerald, author.
Title: Jesuits, theology, and the American Catholic church / Daniel Kendall, SJ, and Gerald O'Collins, SJ.
Description: New York : Paulist Press, 2020. | Includes bibliographical references and index. | Summary: "A historical analysis of the Jesuit influence on American Catholic theology, parish ministries, Biblical studies, education, canon law, spirituality, and ecumenical and interreligious dialogue, especially in the 20th c"— Provided by publisher.
Identifiers: LCCN 2019044795 (print) | LCCN 2019044796 (ebook) | ISBN 9780809155170 (paperback) | ISBN 9781587688898 (ebook)
Subjects: LCSH: Jesuits—Influence. | Catholic Church—United States. Classification: LCC BX1406.3 .K46 2020 (print) | LCC BX1406.3 (ebook) | DDC 282/.730904—dc23
LC record available at https://lccn.loc.gov/2019044795
LC ebook record available at https://lccn.loc.gov/2019044796

ISBN 978-0-8091-5517-0 (paperback)
ISBN 978-1-58768-889-8 (e-book)

Published by Paulist Press
997 Macarthur Boulevard
Mahwah, New Jersey 07430
www.paulistpress.com

Printed and bound in the
United States of America

Daniel Kendall, SJ
Born Miami, Arizona, January 11, 1939;
died Los Gatos, California, May 26, 2020

I first met Dan in Rome when he was a recently ordained Jesuit priest, living at the Collegio Bellarmino and studying for his licentiate in Sacred Scripture at the Pontifical Biblical Institute. He relished life in Rome and delighted in the teaching of Carlo Maria (later Cardinal) Martini and other professors. With his licentiate at the Biblicum finished, he then crossed the street to the Pontifical Gregorian University. He successfully completed a doctorate with me (on several Church fathers applying to purgatory what Paul said in 1 Cor 3:13–15), the first of nearly one hundred students to write and defend a doctoral dissertation with me—my "primogenito," as Dan liked to describe himself.

I began full-time teaching at the Gregorian in 1974, and Dan returned to the United States. He taught at the University of San Francisco from 1979 and, for at least six years, chaired its Department of Theology and Religious Studies. We never lost touch, and for several years Dan hosted me as a visiting professor at the USF summer program. He joined me in writing articles that appeared in *Biblica* (1994), *Catholic Biblical Quarterly* (1992), *Gregorianum* (1993, 1994), *Heythrop Journal* (1996), *Scottish Journal of Theology* (1994), and *Theological Studies* (1987, 1992). Dan built on that experience when he served as book review editor for *Theological Studies* (2012–19).

We started writing and editing books together: *The Bible for Theology* (Paulist Press, 1997); *In Many and Diverse Ways*, a Festschrift in honor of Jacques Dupuis on his eightieth birthday (Orbis, 2003); and four volumes edited with Stephen Davis, published by Oxford University Press and coming from interdisciplinary conferences held in New York, *The Resurrection* (1997), *The Trinity* (1999), *The Incarnation* (2002), and *The Redemption* (2004). With Steve Davis, Dan edited a Festschrift for my seventieth birthday, *The Convergence of Theology* (Paulist Press, 2001). Jeffrey LaBelle joined Dan and I in preparing *Pope John Paul II: A Reader* (Paulist Press, 2007). Then the three of us edited *Seek God Everywhere* (Doubleday, 2010), lectures on the *Spiritual Exercises* delivered by Anthony de Mello. Now the last book that

Dan and I coauthored or coedited, *Jesuits, Theology, and the American Catholic Church*, is about to appear with Paulist Press. In my own name and that of Dan I want to warmly thank the Paulist Press and Senior Academic Editor Donna Crilly.

Dan was the epitome of friendship, encouragement, and fun. Nothing delighted him more than sitting down for a meal with those he loved. I am so glad that in 2019 he was enabled to spend the major part of a sabbatical back at the Collegio Bellarmino, visit his favorite places in Rome, and meet (and be photographed with) Pope Francis. Dan never failed to carefully plan his flights, so that he could catch up with old friends in India, the Philippines, Australia, and elsewhere. Sadly, at the start of March this year the spread of the coronavirus forced him to fly straight home to San Francisco from Manila (via Singapore) rather than make a detour and stay with me in Melbourne.

For nearly fifty years I enjoyed the friendship of Dan and shared him with relatives and others. He was one of the very best friends and academic colleagues I have ever enjoyed. To his sister, Anne, his deceased parents, and the Society of Jesus in the United States, I wish to express my warm thanks for bringing Dan into my life and through him blessing me in so many ways. While I pray for Dan, I am sure he is already delighting in the wonderful, total friendship that is heavenly life, a friendship that will never, never end. RIP.

Those who came to know Dan quickly became conscious of his uncomplicated, deep love for the Society of Jesus and for Jesuits, both at home in the United States and around the world. God's providence has seen to it that his last and posthumous book describes and warmly evaluates what Jesuits have done to develop and share life-giving and truth-enhancing theology in its various branches.

Gerald O'Collins, SJ
Jesuit Theological College, Australia
June 2, 2020

CONTENTS

Preface vii

Abbreviations xv

Chapter 1: The Big Story of Jesuit Influence (1634–2018) 1

Chapter 2: Philosophical Studies and American Jesuits 20

Chapter 3: Theology, Patristics, and Church History 33

Chapter 4: Moral Theology, Liturgy, Pastoral Theology, and Canon Law 52

Chapter 5: Biblical Studies and American Jesuits 71

Chapter 6: Ignatian Spirituality 89

Chapter 7: American Jesuits and the Second Vatican Council 101

Conclusions 119

Notes 123

Index of Names 145

PREFACE

WHAT COUNTS AS "THEOLOGY"? We obviously need to respond to that question before recalling and evaluating the influence that Jesuits, both Americans and others, have exercised in the whole story of theology in the United States from the late eighteenth century until the present.

In a wider sense, all Christian believers are theologians, since they can "give an account" of the faith and love that is "in them" (1 Pet 3:15). In a narrower sense, theology involves a methodical effort to grasp and interpret the truth of God's self-revelation in Jesus Christ. As "faith seeking understanding" (*fides quaerens intellectum*), theology embraces religious education in schools, reflections of parish study groups, the reflections of informed readers, and, preeminently, courses, seminars, and research conducted by teachers and students of academic faculties and departments of theology and religious studies. The "theory" of theology both expresses and shapes the practice of Christian worship and behavior.

From St. Justin Martyr (d. ca. 165) right down to the present, theologians have continued to derive help from some well-based philosophy to clarify critically the concepts, language, questions, and methods they use. What Jesuits in the United States achieved in philosophy has enjoyed its impact also in the theological arena. The 1998 encyclical of St. John Paul II, *Fides et Ratio* (On the Relationship between Faith and Reason), affirms and illustrates that there can be no effective theology without deploying philosophical reason.

The central commitment of theology involves fundamental theology (to be explained), dogmatic or systematic theology, patristics or the study of major writers in the early Church, Church history (which examines the wider Christian tradition, including the history of theology itself), moral theology or Christian ethics, pastoral theology (including liturgy and catechetics), and canon law. Theology will remain feeble or even sterile unless it is constantly "nourished" and "ruled" by the study of the Scriptures, which the Second Vatican Council called "the very soul of sacred theology" (The Constitution on Divine Revelation 21, 24). Outstanding theologians, like St. Thomas Aquinas (ca. 1225–74), have commented on or at least remained in constant contact with the inspired text of the Bible.

Finally, Jesuit theologians have been influenced by Ignatian spirituality and, specifically, the experience of the Spiritual Exercises that have inspired them to remain Jesus-centered and to seek God in all things. The impact of Ignatian spirituality toward developing theology in the United States and elsewhere may resist precise definition. Yet the case of Karl Rahner (1904–84), a German theologian whose influence continues to enrich theology in America and around the world, is emblematic. Those who fail to recognize the role of the Spiritual Exercises cannot grasp fully the genesis and impact of his teaching and writing.

This vision of theology serves as a template for examining the Jesuit influence on the story of Catholic (and Christian) theology in the United States. Chapter 1 will sketch the big picture: it opens with John Carroll (1736–1815), a Jesuit, the first bishop (and then archbishop) of Baltimore, and founder in 1789 of Georgetown Academy. After the Society of Jesus was partially restored in 1806, this institution formally passed into the possession of Jesuits and was raised to the rank of a university by an act of Congress in 1815.

Later landmarks that belong to the Jesuit impact on American theology include the 1869 opening of Woodstock College, the flagship "theologate" twenty-five miles west of Baltimore. That college served as a model for four other Jesuit theologates: Weston College, Weston, Massachusetts (1922 for philosophy, with theology added in 1927); St. Mary's College, St. Mary's, Kansas (created in 1931 when the divinity school of Saint Louis University moved there); Alma College, Alma, California (1934); and West Baden College, West Baden, Indiana (1934).

To these we should add St. Mary of the Lake, Mundelein, Illinois (near Chicago), where Jesuits provided staff from 1921 to 1989. Cardinal George William Mundelein (1872–1939) established this archdiocesan seminary in 1921, and John B. Furay, SJ (1873–1952), moved from being president of Loyola University Chicago to become the prefect of studies of the seminary and, later, dean of the pontifical faculty when the institution was raised to the level of a pontifical university. Edward T. Oakes, SJ (1948–2013), prolonged the Jesuit presence at St. Mary of the Lake by teaching there from 2002 to 2013. He specialized in Christology, grace, and the thought of Hans Urs von Balthasar.

In 1964 West Baden College was renamed the Bellarmine School of Theology (North Aurora, Illinois); it moved into Chicago in 1970 and underwent another change of name (the Jesuit School of Theology in Chicago), only to close in 1981. St. Mary's College migrated back to Saint Louis University in 1967, became Saint Louis University School of Divinity, and closed in 1977. It had enjoyed a notable teacher of moral theology in Gerald Kelly, SJ (1902–64), who published both professional and popular books (including three volumes on medico-moral problems); his practical guide *The Good Confessor* (1962) remains in use.

In 1953 a professor at St. Mary's, Cyril A. Vollert, SJ (1901–80), joined a colleague at Saint Louis University, Gerald F. Van Ackeren, SJ (1916–78), in founding *Theology Digest*. The journal selected and summarized articles from over four hundred theological journals. Each year it also supplied brief information about two hundred or more books and published some lectures. Based at Saint Louis University from 1967, *Theology Digest* lasted until 2010. Van Ackeren was editor from 1953 until 1978.

From the nineteenth into the twentieth century, across the United States Jesuits opened parishes, high schools, colleges, and universities. All of them participated in teaching and transmitting theology to lay alumni and alumnae. Jesuit education and—specifically—theological and philosophical education continues to have an influence on innumerable graduates. Books telling the story of Georgetown University and later foundations spell out this impact on lay graduates.

Nationally and internationally, the Jesuit institutions in the United States have exercised their strongest theological influence through (1) the six faculties of theology (listed above), which are now reduced to two, the Jesuit School of Theology of Santa Clara University and the Boston College School of Theology and Ministry, and (2) the universities and colleges that had graduate programs in theology and philosophy. By 2018, there were fourteen universities and colleges with graduate programs in religious studies and nine with such programs in philosophy.

The early institutions included Fordham University, founded in New York in 1841 and passing into Jesuit hands in 1846, and Marquette University, founded in Milwaukee in 1881. Besides contributing to the progress of theology through such institutions, the Jesuit role in theology was also exercised through publishing books and articles, both academic and popular. Sometimes such books were put out by the publishing houses of Jesuit universities but more often by other publishers. The other houses included Baylor University Press, Catholic University of America Press, Doubleday, Eerdmans, Harvard University Press, Liturgical Press, Oxford University Press, Paulist Press, and Orbis Books—to name only some. *America* magazine (founded in 1909) and *Theological Studies* (founded in 1940) remain highly significant in mediating theology, the former doing so for a wider readership and the latter for teachers and students of theology. Chapter 5 will present another Jesuit journal, *New Testament Abstracts*, that also continues its work. From 1940 to 1992, Fordham University published *Thought*, a quarterly for philosophers, theologians, social activists, and intellectuals of all kinds. The notable contributors included Bernard Lonergan, Jacques Maritain, Thomas Merton, Walker Percy, Karl Rahner, and Elie Wiesel.

Chapter 2 will take up Jesuit commitment to philosophy, which enjoyed an important impact on the development of theology (and philosophy) in the United States. At Fordham University, W. Norris Clarke (1915–2008) for over fifty years taught a brilliant brand of personalist Thomism. At Saint Louis University, Walter Ong (1912–2003) was a stellar figure with his cultural philosophy.

Chapter 3 will explore the influence of Jesuits in the American development of fundamental theology, systematic theology, patristics, and Church history. Here we will recall the work of such theologians as Walter J. Burghardt (1914–2008), Avery Dulles (1918–2008), Francis A. Sullivan (1922–2019), and Jared Wicks (b. 1929). Some of these Jesuits engaged in a many-sided ministry. Burghardt, for example, was not only an outstanding patristic scholar but also for twenty-three years served as editor of *Theological Studies*. In the United States and beyond, he also proved one of the most famous and effective preachers of his generation.

It is not surprising that these are all twentieth-century names.

From the nineteenth century and into the twentieth, neo-Scholasticism (developed at the Gregorian University and elsewhere) and anti-Modernism (promoted by St. Pius X [d. 1914]) inhibited theological development. The first dean of the faculty at Woodstock College, an Italian neo-Scholastic, Camillo (later Cardinal) Mazzella (1833–1900), published three books of dogmatic theology (in Latin), which purported "to teach nothing new" (*nova non docere*). In 1878 he was called to a chair in theology at the Gregorian. He exemplified how at Woodstock and elsewhere American Jesuits studied theology (and often philosophy) through textbooks written in Latin (and often by professors of the Gregorian). Mazzella also initiated the line of non-American Jesuits whose teaching and publishing in the United States affected theology (and philosophy) and sometimes did so in a very positive sense: for instance, Bernard Lonergan (1904–84) and Karl Rahner.

Chapter 4 will examine the place of Jesuits in the history of American moral theology, liturgy, pastoral theology, and canon law. Here it is at our peril that we ignore such figures as John Ford (1902–89), Gerald Kelly (1902–64), Richard McCormick (1922–2000), John Courtney Murray (1904–67), James Keenan (b. 1953), and Ladislas Orsy (b. 1921). This chapter will not neglect the teaching on social justice (including opposition to racism and anti-Semitism) spread by Daniel Lord (1888–1955) and John LaFarge (1880–1963), or the theology of peace developed by Daniel Berrigan (1921–2015).

Chapter 5 will attend to the influence of American Jesuits, like Joseph A. Fitzmyer (1920–2016), Richard J. Clifford (b. 1934), Daniel Harrington (1940–2014), exercised on biblical studies in the United States (and beyond). Fitzmyer's eminence was recognized not only by his being elected president of three major organizations, the Catholic Biblical Association of America (1969/70), the Society of Biblical Literature (1979), and the Studiorum Novi Testamenti Societas (1992), but also by his editing for a time the journals of the first two organizations: *The Catholic Biblical Quarterly* and *The Journal of Biblical Literature*. Once again, we should not ignore the contribution made by non-American Jesuits who visited the United States to lecture on the Scriptures: for instance, Luis Alonso-Schökel (1920–98) and Cardinal Carlo Maria Martini (1927–2012).

Chapter 6 turns to the practical theological influence that Jesuits exercised across the country through their retreat centers, which enabled innumerable laypeople, priests, religious, and bishops to make the Spiritual Exercises, right up to their full form of thirty days. After its foundation in St. Louis in 1968, the American Assistancy Seminar on Jesuit Spirituality brought Jesuit history and Ignatian spirituality to life for innumerable people in the United States and beyond, above all through its *Studies in the Spirituality of Jesuits*. In 2014 the center moved to Boston and became the Boston College Institute of Advanced Jesuit Research. From 1962, summer programs at the University of San Francisco also did much to encourage spirituality in theology and pastoral ministry. So too did summer programs at other Jesuit universities and colleges in the United States.

Numerous non-American Jesuits came on visits and shared in this promotion of Ignatian spirituality. The most significant of these visitors has, undoubtedly, been Pope Francis, whose 2015 apostolic pilgrimage to the United States helped spread Ignatian spirituality. It has shone through his preaching, governance, the apostolic exhortation *Evangelii Gaudium* (The Joy of the Gospel, 2013), and other major documents.

This book would be seriously deficient if it failed to investigate in chapter 7 what Jesuits like John O'Malley and Jared Wicks did toward receiving and implementing the teaching and decisions of the Second Vatican Council (1962–65). Here we also pay attention to Jesuit involvement in dialogues with "others" promoted by the Council. Wicks, for instance, was very prominent in the meetings with Lutherans, which produced the landmark document of 1999, the "Joint Declaration on the Doctrine of Justification."

The concluding chapter will draw together this polyvalent story of Jesuit influence on theology in the United States, an influence exercised by institutions and individuals and through teaching, writing, and organizing. Inevitably this book must be selective and will pass over individuals and events that could enter a fuller account of the Jesuit impact on American theology. We may well have committed some glaring omissions; for these we apologize in advance.

This book sets itself to describe and evaluate the Jesuit influence on the history of American theology, primarily but not exclusively Catholic theology. In no way does it wish to deny or downplay the influence on that history exercised by (a) men and women who belonged to other religious institutes, (b) diocesan priests, and (c) laypersons. A Sulpician, Raymond E. Brown (1928–98), enjoyed a huge influence on the development of New Testament studies in the United States and beyond. David

Tracy (b. 1939), a diocesan priest, made a lasting contribution to issues in fundamental theology, as did John Tracy Ellis (1905–92) to church history. John T. Noonan (1926–2017), a layman, helped to shape the story of moral theology, while Dorothy Day (1897–1975), a laywoman, encouraged the development of Catholic peace studies.

Tracy reminds us of how difficult it can be to sharply define Jesuit influence. He studied theology with the Jesuits at the Gregorian University in Rome, up to a doctorate in 1969. Early in his career he wrote a landmark study on the Jesuit philosopher-theologian Bernard Lonergan: *The Achievement of Bernard Lonergan* (New York: Herder & Herder, 1970). That book also reveals something of the thought of an outstanding Jesuit theologian of the twentieth century, Karl Rahner. The wide influence exercised by Tracy's theological reflection is, in some sense, a Jesuit-inspired influence.

We use the terminology of Old Testament (OT) and New Testament (NT). Here "old" is understood as good and does not imply "supersessionism," the view that the New Testament has rendered obsolete the Old Testament and so "superseded" it.

Throughout this book, for the sake of clarity, we add the postnominal "SJ." In a work essentially concerned with Jesuits, we need to do that. But such practice is in no way intended to "put down" women and men who belong to other religious institutes and are cited without their postnominals being added.

For various kinds of help in writing this book, we warmly thank William A. Barry, SJ, Christopher Bellitto, Brendan Byrne, SJ, Louis Caruana, SJ, Charlotte Clements, Richard Clifford, SJ, Brian E. Daley, SJ, Isaac Demase, SJ, Robert Doran, SJ, Harry J. Gensler, SJ, Justin Glyn, SJ, Dinh Trung Hoa, SJ, Leon Hooper, SJ, James F. Keenan, SJ, Robin Koning, SJ, Joseph W. Koterski, SJ, Daniel Madigan, SJ, James J. Martin, SJ, John Martis, SJ, Joseph McAuley, Shannon McMillen-Evans, David Miros, William Muller, SJ, Ladislas Orsy, SJ, John W. Padberg, SJ, Daniel Peterson, SJ, Oliver Rafferty, SJ, Thomas J. Regan, SJ, William R. Rehg, SJ, Paul Rourke, SJ, Ormond Rush, Stephen R. Schloesser, SJ, Michael Sheeran, SJ, Simon Smith, SJ, Geoff Thomson, Sabine Voermans (and other staff members of the Dalton McCaughey Library), and Jared Wicks, SJ. We dedicate this book to all those Jesuits in the United States who have shared with us their theological ministry.

Daniel Kendall, SJ, and Gerald O'Collins, SJ

ABBREVIATIONS

CEJ: Thomas Worcester, ed., *The Cambridge Encyclopedia of the Jesuits* (Cambridge, UK: Cambridge University Press, 2017).

JCP: Thomas O. Hanley, ed., *The John Carroll Papers*, 3 vols. (Notre Dame, IN: University of Notre Dame Press, 1976).

NT: New Testament

OT: Old Testament

TS: *Theological Studies* (1940–)

CHAPTER 1

THE BIG STORY OF JESUIT INFLUENCE (1634–2018)

JESUITS WERE PRESENT in the American colonies from 1634, when on March 25, the Feast of the Annunciation, two priests and one brother arrived on the *Ark* and the *Dove* from England with the original cohort of seventeen gentlemen (mostly Catholics) and around two hundred laborers and servants (mostly Protestants) and settled in Maryland. Up to 1773, when the Society of Jesus was suppressed by Pope Clement XIV, 156 Jesuits served on the Maryland Mission; in the year of the Society's dissolution, twenty-three Jesuits belonged to that mission. Like Archbishop John Carroll (1736–1815), who had been born in Maryland, they were all educated in Europe.[1] Carroll died a year after the official restoration of the Society in North America and around the world (1814). He had prepared its future ministry of education, including theological education, through the foundation of Georgetown University. In sketching major outlines of the Jesuit influence on theology in the United States, this opening chapter first takes up the story of Carroll, who was also the founder of the Catholic hierarchy in the United States.[2]

ARCHBISHOP JOHN CARROLL

John Carroll was born into an elite Catholic family that enjoyed wealth, education, and social prominence. After studying for two years at a local Jesuit school (Bohemia Manor Academy on the Chesapeake Bay), in 1748 he sailed for Europe to complete his secondary education at St. Omer College, Flanders. Discerning a call to religious life, in 1753 he entered the Society of Jesus.[3] After completing the novitiate, he did his Jesuit training in Liège. He was ordained a priest in 1769 and apparently took final vows in 1771.[4] Already in February 1769, a letter to his brother Daniel shows a deep concern about the future of the Jesuits. Their protector, Pope Clement XIII, had died, having resisted to the end the governments of France, Naples, Portugal, and Spain, which demanded the immediate dissolution of the Society of Jesus. The "atrocious falsehoods, injustices, cruelties, and mean artifices employed against us" made Carroll fear the worst from the coming papal conclave. Lorenzo Ganganelli, elected pope on May 18, 1769, would, as Clement XIV, decree the universal suppression of the Jesuits on July 21, 1773.[5]

A grand tour of Europe[6] brought Carroll to Rome (October 1772–June 1773), a "traumatic experience" that left him with a "lasting low opinion of Clement XIV."[7] Writing from Rome on January 23, 1773, to an English Jesuit friend, he declared that "our catastrophe is near at hand" and remarked on "the toleration allowed here to everything done or said against us." In a letter to the same friend of February 3, 1773, he spoke of "the gloom which overspreads us here at Rome." He mentioned how "the Cardinal Visitor" had forbidden "under pain of excommunication" a Mass that was being said every day at the altar of St. Francis Xavier in the Church of the Gesù. Carroll added, "The strange sanction surprised everybody, and appears very irregular for the very first notice sent to the administrators." He went on to talk of "another very serious affair here," namely, that "the presses swarm with writings against the devotion to the Sacred Heart." He acknowledged the challenge to his own belief in the papal leadership of the Church: "What a revolution of ideas do all these proceedings produce in a mind accustomed to regard this city as the seat of religion and the bulwark against the encroachments of irreligion and impiety!"[8]

A week after Carroll, now back in Bruges, received the news of the Society's suppression, he wrote to his mother on September 11, 1773: "I am not, and perhaps never shall be, recovered from the shock of this dreadful intelligence." He could not understand how divine providence could allow the termination of a religious institute "wholly devoted to procuring every comfort and advantage to their neighbors, whether by preaching, teaching, catechizing, missions, visiting hospitals, prisons, and every other function of spiritual and corporal mercy."[9] In the event, Carroll was to play a role in the worldwide restoration of the Society and its resuming those works of mercy.

In 1774, Carroll returned to the home of his family in Maryland, engaged in pastoral work among the Catholics of that colony, and shared in the 1776 Declaration of Independence and its aftermath in the American Constitution of 1789 and the Bill of Rights of 1791. His cousin Charles was a signatory, the only Catholic signatory, of the Declaration of Independence. His older brother Daniel would sign the Constitution on behalf of the state of Maryland. He himself became a friend of one of the leading Founding Fathers, Benjamin Franklin (1706–90). In April 1776, he joined Franklin and two other commissioners as an adviser for a mission to Canada on behalf of the Continental Congress, which hoped to gain Canadian support for American independence.[10] His friendship with Franklin contributed to Carroll's being appointed as bishop—specifically through Franklin's subsequent contacts in Paris with the papal nuncio. After Franklin returned from his years in Paris (1776–85) as commissioner for the United States, John Carroll wrote to him on April 2, 1787: "I esteem it one of the most fortunate and honourable events of my life that I had an opportunity of forming an acquaintance with you, and I flatter myself with having inspired you with some sentiments of regard and more than general benevolence towards me."[11]

What John Carroll achieved in American history marks him out as one of the most outstanding of all the ex-Jesuits who were left bereft and adrift after their brutal suppression. Through the 1780s he emerged as a leader among the Catholics of Maryland. He became bishop (1789–1808) and then archbishop (1808–15) of Baltimore, being "the first and last bishop chosen in the United States by an electoral body made up of all the clergy."[12] He was also the first Catholic bishop in the United States, with his diocese originally extending from the Canadian border to the Gulf of Mexico and from Chesapeake Bay to the Mississippi. His influence on subsequent American theology touched at least four areas: church-state relations, education, communion with the Bishop of Rome, and doctrines and devotions concerning the Blessed Virgin Mary and the Sacred Heart of Jesus. We take up these areas in turn.

(1) For Carroll, the independence of the American colonies should involve (a) the right of all citizens to follow their

conscience and practice publicly the faith they espouse[13] and (b) an appropriate separation of church and state. Hence, the appointment of Catholic bishops should not depend either on the U.S. Congress or on decisions of the states. There was to be no established church; civil unity did not entail religious uniformity. Carroll himself consistently pursued peaceful relations between Christian denominations and hoped that this situation would characterize the new republic. His ancestors had fled persecution and a Europe torn asunder by wars between Catholics and Protestants. In a letter to Franklin, dated January 18, 1778, he summed up the American dream of civil and religious liberty, developed from the colonial and revolutionary experience, as the "new order of things, a new combination of ideas and pursuits, indeed…*the new world*."[14] Writing to Cardinal Vitaliano Borromeo on November 10, 1783, he declared that "in these United States our religious system has undergone a revolution, if possible, more extraordinary than our political one. In all of them, free toleration is allowed to Christians of every denomination…a communication of all civil rights, without distinction or diminution, is extended to those of our religion."[15] In the mid-twentieth century the questions of conscience and religious freedom were taken up famously by the Jesuit theologian, John Courtney Murray. But, somewhat curiously, Murray paid little or no attention to Carroll in a landmark work, *We Hold These Truths: Catholic Reflections on the American Proposition*.[16] Murray had prepared himself for this classic study by writing for *TS* (1952–54) a five-part study on church and state in the teaching of Pope Leo XIII.

Pursuing harmony with other Christian churches, Carroll bequeathed an early ecumenical spirit of religious toleration. He understood his Protestant neighbors to be members of the same Church, even if not, or not yet, in communion with him. Before the Second Vatican Council took place, these intimations would come into their own not only across the United States but also, specifically, at Woodstock College on the edge of Baltimore. John Courtney Murray's colleague, Gustave Weigel, SJ (1906–64), led the way through working with such Protestant churchmen as Robert McAfee Brown (1920–2001), who was to be appointed a Presbyterian observer at Vatican II. Murray himself became the principal architect of Vatican II's Declaration on Religious Freedom, an essential part of the Maryland tradition stemming from Carroll.

(2) The Jesuit commitment to education encouraged Carroll to found in 1789 Georgetown University, as it officially became in 1815. The original building was not ready until late 1791. The first student arrived in November 1791 and classes started in the following January. Emmett Curran remarks, "Carroll had founded Georgetown at the very creation of the institutional American church [Carroll's election as bishop of Baltimore], in order that it might grow in wisdom and truth in a republic that depended for its survival on a free and educated citizenry."[17] A 1787 letter by Carroll to an English friend, also a former Jesuit, set out at length "the two great undertakings on hand, for the success of which we stand in need of every support and best advice from the friends of religion. We have resolved to establish an academy for the education of youth, and to solicit the appointment of a diocesan bishop." "The latter," he added, "is a necessary consequence of the former.... The establishment of an academy is to form subjects capable of becoming useful members of the ministry; and to these a bishop for ordination will be indispensably necessary."[18] Carroll wanted Georgetown University to prepare candidates for clerical training (to be offered at a seminary in Baltimore) and to provide young men of all faiths with a classical liberal arts education that included English, French, Greek, Latin, mathematics, philosophy, and rhetoric.[19] The curriculum that he envisaged followed the *Ratio Studiorum*, the system of education Jesuits first promulgated in 1599 and revised in 1832.

Regarding religious instruction at Georgetown,[20] in the 1940s John Courtney Murray became involved in sketching a distinctive program that would be integrated with the religious formation of students.[21] But his planning came to nothing.[22] Political and social upheavals in American life during World War II and its aftermath, the impetus given by Vatican II (1962–65) toward openness to other Christians and other religions, the development of biblical studies (with a distinction between what scriptural texts meant then and what they can mean now), and other factors put an end to the notion of an organized body of truths to be learned by all students, or at least by all Catholic students. Changes in the curriculum reduced required courses and introduced more electives in scriptural studies, Christian ethics, the theology of religions, and foundational courses that led students into the mystery of God.

Eventually there would be twenty-eight Jesuit universities and colleges in the United States.[23] Through their departments of theology and religious studies, those institutions all contributed to theological developments, even if for many years the five theologates (starting with the opening of Woodstock College in 1869) and the faculty at Mundelein were to remain in the forefront. But by the start of the third millennium, the Jesuits had ceased to teach at Mundelein and the five theologates had been reduced to two, with both of them incorporated into Jesuit universities: Alma College after its 1969 move to Berkeley united with Santa Clara University, and Weston College with Boston College. Along with the universities and colleges, American Jesuits were to found numerous high schools, often closely associated with one of their institutions of higher education. These high schools taught religious education and helped shape the practice of catechetics in the United States. So too did the prominent Jesuit parishes associated with almost all their universities and colleges, Fordham University in New York and Holy Cross College in Worcester among the few exceptions not having such a parish. In the United States, Carroll was the founder and pioneer of Jesuit eduction and, in particular, its philosophical and theological emphasis.[24]

(3) Despite experiencing firsthand the sordid events leading to the worldwide suppression of the Society of Jesus, including what happened in Rome on the very eve of the papal brief of suppression (July 21, 1773), John Carroll remained true to the Petrine leadership of the Catholic Church. The

experience of the birth of the American republic encouraged him to seek a measure of autonomy of the local church from Roman decision-making. But he never wavered in upholding Catholic unity "with and under" Peter. He sent seminarians to be educated in Rome by the *Propaganda Fide*, which contributed funds toward the establishment of the academy in Georgetown (from 1815, Georgetown University). He expected that not only seminarians but also Catholic lay students who attended Georgetown would learn "zeal, pure faith, and inevitable fidelity to the Holy See."[25] Leaving aside the question of whether the pope is infallible "even without a council," he maintained clearly that the Church's infallibility "resides in the body of bishops united and agreeing with their head, the bishop of Rome."[26] Carroll tied his episcopal authority to that of the See of Peter: "To the Vicar of Christ we owe obedience in things purely spiritual." The "Successor of Peter is the visible head" and "chief pastor" of the Church, to whom "true obedience" is to be given.[27]

(4) We saw how shocked the young Carroll was by hostility in Rome toward devotion to the Sacred Heart of Jesus. That devotion along with the Marian devotion that he experienced on visits to the Duke of Norfolk and other aristocratic Catholic families in England shaped his spirituality and his ministry. As a Marylander, he remembered that the first settlers came ashore on the Feast of the Annunciation. He chose Mary the Mother of God as patroness of the diocese, was consecrated the first bishop of Baltimore on the Feast of the Assumption, and named the first cathedral church the Cathedral of the Assumption.

Shortly after Pius XII solemnly defined in 1950 the doctrine of Mary's Assumption, a Jesuit professor at Fordham University, Paul F. Palmer, published *Mary in the Documents of the Church.*[28] Before citing various historical texts on Mary's Assumption, Palmer noted how Carroll had dedicated the primatial see of Baltimore to "our Lady of the Assumption."[29] Palmer later published a collection of essays, *A Theology of Mary* (1965). He and other Jesuit theologians, by encouraging devotion to Mary and the Sacred Heart, stood in a tradition that went back to Carroll.

This summary of Carroll's views and achievements dwells on his earlier years. Raymond Schroth shows how Carroll's more liberal vision became mitigated in his later years.[30]

FOUNDATION OF WOODSTOCK COLLEGE

Even before the death of Archbishop Carroll in 1815, Jesuits around the world were engaged in the task of rebuilding their ministries, including that of teaching and developing philosophy and theology. After the ravages of the American Civil War (April 1861 to May 1865), a major landmark in this development was the foundation in 1869 on the outskirts of Baltimore of the first major Jesuit theologate in the United States, Woodstock College.[31] Up to that point, scholastics, as Jesuit students in training are called, studied philosophy and theology at Georgetown University, at Fordham University, or briefly, in Boston. Now they were to be brought together in a separate house of studies for American scholastics, modelled on such houses in Europe.

Woodstock College was built in the beautiful countryside. Schroth describes the setting: "The woods were lush with cedar, oak, hickory, and maple trees and the river slopes with laurel that the seminarians would gather at Christmastime. The quarry from which they would hew granite for the house would, over the century, fill with water in which the men would swim. But the institutional building and its surroundings had a downside: according to legend, one Italian professor looked up at the imposing, four-story, rectangular structure surrounded by hills and woods and said: '*aut studium aut suicidium* (they'll either study or kill themselves).'"[32]

The eight professors who constituted the original teaching staff were all non-Americans: one German, one Spaniard, one Swiss, and five Italians—all made available by persecutions that drove them from their own countries.[33] Camillo Mazzella and three other Italians had already taught at Georgetown University before moving with part of the library and several scholastics to Woodstock in the Maryland countryside. Mazzella, Woodstock's first prefect of studies and first professor of dogmatic theology, "looked like a tower of orthodoxy, always seeking truth for its own sake, always following in the footsteps of approved authors."[34] Latin was the language of instruction, and it was in Latin that Mazzella composed the earliest theological works to be published by a Woodstock professor (and through Woodstock's own press): *De Deo creante* (On God Creating, 1877) and *De Gratia Christi* (On the Grace of Christ, 1878). His *De Virtutibus infusis* (On the Infused Virtues) was published in Rome in 1879, a year after Pope Leo XIII called Mazzella to a chair in theology at the Gregorian University in Rome. Mazzella was created a cardinal in 1886 and then in 1897 was appointed the cardinal archbishop of Palestrina, where he served until his death in 1900. At Woodstock, manuals written in Latin and often by Gregorian professors would continue to provide the textbooks well into the twentieth century.

The solitary Spaniard on the original Woodstock faculty, Carlos M. Maldonado, arrived after having taught theology for eleven years in Salamanca, where "he presided in the chair once occupied by the great Suárez, his idol and his model."[35] From the late nineteenth century, Suárezianism gradually declined in the aftermath of Pope Leo XIII's bull *Aeterni Patris* (Of the Eternal Father, 1879), which encouraged all theology students to study the philosophy and theology of St. Thomas Aquinas. Our next chapter returns to this development.

Carlo Piccirillo (1821–88) was a notable librarian. He came to Woodstock after contributing for years to *Civiltà Cattolica*, a Jesuit journal founded in 1850, published in Rome, and serving as the unofficial voice of the Holy See. During his eleven years running Woodstock's library, Piccirillo added over ten thousand new books (mainly in Latin and English).

In 1833, the Holy See authorized Georgetown University to grant pontifical degrees in philosophy and theology. As William McFadden reports, "The Jesuit superior general, Jan Roothaan, had petitioned for this authority from Pope Gregory XVI. Roothaan argued that this would make Georgetown the only university in the United States to grant a doctorate in Catholic theology." Consequently, "young ecclesiastics allured by the hope of the doctorate, which is highly esteemed in these states, would gather there from all directions, and thus make thoroughly the course of theology, which they now make superficially in their dioceses."[36] While studying separately after 1869, Woodstock scholastics continued to receive their degrees from Georgetown. In his 1891 *Memorial of the First Century of Georgetown College, D.C.: Comprising a History of Georgetown University*, John G. Shea remarked:

Woodstock "is really at present the Theological Department of Georgetown University."[37] In 1897, the president of Georgetown, John Havens Richards, SJ, called the decision to set up Woodstock "a grave error of policy" not only for Georgetown but also for Woodstock itself. He explained, "The professors and students were transported to a semi-wilderness, remote from libraries, from contact with the learned world, and from all those stimulating influences which affect intellectual life in large centers of population and culture."[38]

Despite this "remoteness," Woodstock played a role in the spirituality of Catholic Americans—in particular, through continuing to spread devotion to the Sacred Heart. In 1792 some ex-Jesuits in Georgetown had produced *The Pious Guide to Prayer and Devotion*, which proved popular among lay Catholics; by 1852 it had gone through at least twelve editions. It strongly encouraged devotion to the Sacred Heart of Jesus.[39] Writing on June 17, 1793, to Cardinal Leonardo Antonelli (*Propaganda Fide*), Bishop Carroll assured him that devotion to the Sacred Heart of Jesus "has enjoyed great favour here for many years. I very greatly desire that the Mass and Office of the Sacred Heart be permitted to all on the Friday after the octave of Corpus Christi."[40] Founded at Georgetown College in 1866, *The Messenger of the Sacred Heart* moved to Woodstock when it opened three years later. Within a few months of its first issue, the circulation of *The Messenger* had already topped two thousand. It went on to become one of the most popular magazines of Catholic piety. Even more popular was the Apostleship of Prayer, an association for practicing and spreading devotion to the Sacred Heart among laypeople, as well as among religious, priests, and seminarians. From the 1850s, parish missions gave Jesuits a further means for promulgating devotion to the Sacred Heart, especially through establishing the Confraternities of the Apostleship of Prayer.[41]

At Woodstock itself, the house was formally consecrated to the Sacred Heart in 1873, the year in which a large statue of the Sacred Heart was erected on the grounds. A grotto of Our Lady of Lourdes followed in 1877.

Did the Woodstock Jesuits or, for that matter, other American Jesuits publish anything that contributed to developing academic or popular theology in the United States prior to the end of the First World War? From the opening of Woodstock in 1869 until 1918, *the* most influential work in American theological literature was the 1885

Baltimore Catechism, the official national catechism prepared at the Third Council of Baltimore and widely used even as late as the 1960s. Eventually it was officially replaced in 2004 by the *United States Catholic Catechism for Adults*, based on the revised *Catechism of the Catholic Church* (1997). The *Baltimore Catechism* was drafted by an Italian diocesan priest who belonged to the Diocese of Newark (New Jersey), Januarius Vincent de Concilio (1836–98). Jesuits were involved, or rather a Jesuit was involved, in its production, since this catechism was based on the 1614 *Small Catechism* of St. Robert Bellarmine (1542–1621). In 1892 Georgetown University awarded de Concilio the degree of Doctor of Divinity.

Creative writing came through edifying fiction and some works in medical ethics. One Midwest Jesuit, Francis J. Finn (1859–1928), produced for young people twenty-seven novels that inculcated moral precepts. Another Jesuit, Henry Stanislaus Spalding (1865–1934), became known for his edifying adventure books for boys. He also wrote several books on medical ethics, connected with his part in establishing at Marquette University (1903–8) what is now the Medical School of Wisconsin. In 1911 he also helped set up in Chicago the Loyola University School of Medicine, now the Stritch School of Medicine. In 1892 Creighton University, Omaha, established what became its School of Medicine. In 1849 Georgetown had established a medical department, also later called the School of Medicine. Saint Louis University began medical studies even earlier—in 1836. More input on medical ethics came to the United States with works by the Belgian Jesuit Charles Coppens (1835–1920). In 1896 Coppens published *A Brief Text-book of Moral Philosophy* (reprinted as a paperback in 2016) and in 1897 *Moral Principles and Medical Practice: The Basis of Medical Jurisprudence* (paperback, 2013). The five schools of medicine established by American Jesuits in the nineteenth and early twentieth centuries necessarily called for some teaching and publishing in medical ethics. This was the start of (academic and practical) moral theology developed by Jesuits in the United States. Coppens contributed the entry on "abortion" for volume 1 of the 1913 *Catholic Encyclopedia*.

Published in fifteen volumes, the *Catholic Encyclopedia* had five editors, one of whom was a Jesuit, John J. Wynne. There were also Jesuit contributors to what was, up to that point, the greatest monument of American Catholic learning. Volume 1, for instance, contained entries from six Jesuits at Woodstock and from four Jesuits at

Saint Louis University. Besides Coppens, Jesuits from other countries were also contributors to volume 1: for example, Herbert Thurston from London wrote such entries as "Agnus Dei," "Aliturgical Days," and on various medieval saints (e.g., St. Aelred of Rievaulx, St. Aldegundis, St. Aldhelm, St. Alfrida, and St. Alfwold).

NEO-SCHOLASTICISM AND MODERNISM

For many years, theological textbooks (or "manuals")[42] produced in Rome, Austria (e.g., the works of Ludwig Lercher, SJ [1864–1937]), Spain (e.g., the *Biblioteca de Autores Cristianos*), and elsewhere often exemplified "uniformity and stagnation."[43] They belonged to the era of neo-Scholasticism, a revival of medieval philosophy and theology regularly considered synonymous with neo-Thomism but, in fact, somewhat wider in its content and method. At the Roman College (renamed the Gregorian University) Jesuits such as Luigi Taparelli d'Azeglio (1793–1862), Matteo Liberatore (1810–92), Joseph Kleutgen (1811–93), and Johann Baptist Franzelin (1816–86) began to restore the Scholasticism of the Middle Ages. One of Taparelli's former students, Gioacchino Pecci (1810–1903), as bishop of Perugia and later as Pope Leo XIII, decisively encouraged the movement. His 1879 encyclical *Aeterni Patris* prescribed the teaching of Thomism in Catholic faculties.[44] Up to the Second Vatican Council, neo-Scholasticism helped to give a structure and clarity to Catholic theological thought.

But progress in biblical, historical, liturgical, and patristic studies showed the clarity of neo-Scholasticism to be at times merely formal and lacking in substance. Developments in philosophy also affected theology and, in particular, the dominance of Thomism. Such fresh currents as existentialism, linguistic analysis, personalism, and process thought established a new situation of pluralism.

Where neo-Scholasticism shaped from within the theology that several generations of American Jesuits learned and taught, the papal condemnation of "Modernism" hovered over them as "the sum of all heresies" (St. Pius X) with which they must not trifle. *Modernism* was an umbrella term for a rather diffuse theological movement of the late nineteenth and early twentieth centuries, found in England, France,

Italy, and, to some extent, Germany. Among its main representatives were Alfred Loisy (1857–1940), George Tyrrell (1861–1909), and, perhaps, Baron Friedrich von Hügel (1852–1925).[45] Modernists endorsed contemporary biblical criticism, accepted historical developments in Christianity, strongly opposed neo-Scholasticism, and were thoroughly receptive to progress in science and philosophy. In 1907 through the decree *Lamentabili* (which rejected sixty-five propositions taken from the Modernists) and the encyclical *Pascendi*, Pius X condemned Modernism but in a way that failed to make careful distinctions. A subsequent campaign hunted down those suspected of Modernist tendencies. Pius XII's 1943 encyclical on biblical criticism, *Divino Afflante Spiritu*, the Second Vatican Council, and other developments in church teaching and theology vindicated some, but not all, of the views of the Modernists. In what they wrote about continuing revelation and dogmatic formulae changing their meaning, they could be less than precise.

DANIEL LORD, JOHN LaFARGE, AND BEYOND

In the late nineteenth century and early twentieth century, the United States witnessed an extraordinary growth in the Catholic Church and the Society of Jesus. Between 1880 and 1920, around a million Catholics poured into the United States every decade. Jesuits played their role in providing for and assimilating these waves of migrants by establishing and running parishes, residences, schools, colleges, and universities. But from the early nineteenth century, Jesuits had already been heavily involved in evangelization, teaching, and parish ministries in the Midwest, the Pacific Northwest, California, and New Mexico.[46]

In chronological order, Midwestern Jesuits administered residences or quasi-residences for a longer or shorter time in the following locations: St. Charles, MO (1828); Florissant, MO (1832); Portage de Sioux, MO (1835); Westphalia, MO (1838); Washington, MO (1838); St. Michel, LA (1840); St. Francis Xavier on the Willamette, OR (1844); St. Joseph's, St. Louis, MO (1846); Chillicothe, OH (1847); Cahokia, IL (1847); Newport, KY (1848); Dardenne, MO (1848); Bronsgrove (White Oak), OH (1848); Green Bay, WI (1849);

Manitowoc Rapids, WI (1851); Milwaukee, WI (1855); Normandy, MO (1855); Chicago, IL (1857). The residences in Milwaukee and Chicago evolved into colleges and then universities.

After their restoration, Jesuits also resumed their missions among the Native Americans.[47] In 1841, a party of Jesuits crossed the Rockies and, on the right bank of the Bitter Root River, they set up St. Mary's Mission among the Flatheads, the first Catholic mission in the Pacific Northwest. The most important mission opened by Jesuits among the Rocky Mountain tribes was St. Ignatius of Kalispel, a lasting monument to the zeal of Peter John De Smet, SJ (1801–73).[48] Jesuits opened schools, building them in the heart of Native American country. This differed from the practice of locating boarding schools outside reservations to promote Native American absorption of white culture.

In 1851, one of De Smet's recruits, Michele Accolti, SJ, established a permanent Jesuit presence in California by taking over the buildings of Mission Santa Clara and founding a boarding college, which grew to become Santa Clara University in 1912. After the European revolutions of 1848, staffing was supplied by Italian Jesuits who arrived in increased numbers. By 1873, Jesuits were running schools in Bernalillo, Albuquerque, Las Vegas, and Santa Fe and along the upper Rio Grande Valley. Public schools in at least five counties of New Mexico were staffed by Jesuits and members of other religious institutes.

With this heavy commitment to earlier and later European migrants and to the Indian missions, Jesuits contributed little to the development of theological thinking. Apart from their input in the area of popular spirituality, for many years Jesuit theologians and biblical professors largely remained in the static world of neo-Scholasticism and were inhibited by Pius X's condemnation of Modernism. Interestingly, years later some Jesuits were to share in a scholarly reassessment of the Modernists.[49]

For decades little creativity showed up in American Jesuit theology, except for the area of social ethics. Responding to the official social teaching inaugurated by the 1891 encyclical of Leo XIII, *Rerum Novarum*, and social questions raised by the Great Depression, Daniel Lord, SJ, through his Summer Schools for Catholic Action, encouraged social justice and a ministry among the poor. John LaFarge, SJ, a Harvard graduate who spoke fluent French and German, enjoyed in his earlier years a priestly ministry in rural and urban areas, with rich and poor, Catholics and non-Catholics, blacks and whites. He campaigned not only against communism and fascism but also for civil rights in society, interracial justice, and an end to social barriers within the Church.[50] He enjoyed an editorial platform in *America* magazine, and on the eve of World War II prepared for Pius XI an encyclical condemning racism and antisemitism, *Humani Generis Unitas* (the Unity of the Human Race), which, due to the pope's death in February 1939, was never published.[51]

In 1940, *Theological Studies* began to appear and has been a flagship of Jesuit theology in the United States and beyond. It enjoyed two influential and long-serving editors in John Courtney Murray, SJ, and Walter Burghardt, SJ. The former was editor in chief from 1941 to 1967, and the latter was editor in chief from 1967 to 1990. While *Theological Studies* remains firmly in Jesuit hands, many of the contributors have not been Jesuits. For American Jesuits themselves, *Theological Studies* has not been the only outlet for publishing articles. Their articles have appeared in *Horizons* (the journal of the College Theological Society), the *Proceedings of the Catholic Theological Society*, *Thought* (until it closed in 1992), and other American theological journals, as well as in such European journals as the *Gregorianum*, *Heythrop Journal*, and the *Irish Theological Quarterly*. While *Theological Studies* was beginning its fruitful years of contribution to Catholic theology, four papal encyclicals had their impact—not always a positive one.

Pius XII in his 1943 encyclical *Divino Afflante Spiritu* opened the way for critical biblical scholarship, and his 1947 encyclical *Mediator Dei* brought some reforms in liturgical practice and studies. But his 1943 encyclical *Mystici Corporis* identified the Mystical Body of Christ with the Roman Catholic Church and used the term "church" exclusively of the Roman Catholic Church. Then a 1950 encyclical, *Humani Generis*, described the work of theologians as primarily that of expounding and defending the current teaching of the pope: "It is for them to show how the teaching of the living Magisterium is found in the Sacred Scriptures and in the divine tradition, whether explicitly or implicitly" (art. 21).

This encyclical was widely and correctly understood to repudiate the *ressourcement* approach of the *Nouvelle Théologie* of French Dominicans (like Yves Congar) and Jesuits (like Jean Daniélou and Henri de Lubac). Their theology used a "genetic" method, a return to the sources that studied first the biblical witness and then the subsequent history of doctrinal development. By starting from the Scriptures and the fathers, it tracked, along the lines of John Henry Newman's view of development, the living tradition and what it embodied for growth and change in the Church's teaching and practice. From 1942, Daniélou, his colleagues, and his successors had contributed to the patristic revival by beginning to edit (with appropriate notes and introduction) a series of patristic and medieval texts, *Sources Chrétiennes*. By 2018 the series included 596 works.[52]

VATICAN II—BEFORE, DURING, AND AFTER

Among American Jesuits, Walter J. Burghardt (1914–2008) led the patristic movement, publishing work on such fathers of the Church as Augustine of Hippo and Cyril of Alexandria, teaching historical theology for thirty-two years at Woodstock College, and serving as senior fellow at the Woodstock Theological Center of Georgetown University (1974–2003). For twenty-three years he was editor in chief of the quarterly *Theological Studies*. An outstanding preacher, he broke open the word of God and prophetically denounced the terrible injustices suffered by the poor, blacks, Hispanics, women, and children. The twenty-three honorary doctorates he received from colleges and universities across the United States witness to the pervasive theological and pastoral influence he enjoyed.[53]

The 1943 encyclical of Pius XII, *Divino Afflante Spiritu*, encouraged the scholarly work of the Biblical Institute in Rome (founded 1909) and the École Biblique in Jerusalem (founded 1890). American programs contributed to forming Jesuit leaders in scriptural studies. Several among them studied at Harvard's center of Near Eastern Languages and Literature. Joseph A. Fitzmyer, SJ (1920–2016), however, took his doctorate in Semitic studies at Johns Hopkins University in Baltimore. He will be remembered for his contributions to the study of the Dead Sea Scrolls and for his commentaries on Luke, Acts, Romans, and 1 Corinthians in the Anchor Bible series. He was one of the three general editors of the highly successful *Jerome Biblical Commentary* (both the original edition of 1968 and the second, revised edition of 1989, *The New Jerome Biblical Commentary*). The *JBC* and the *NJBC* testified to the growth of American Catholic scriptural scholarship and to the part Jesuits played in that story. The *JBC* included eleven Jesuit contributors, and the *NJBC* included sixteen Jesuit contributors. After its foundation in 1939, Jesuit experts wrote frequently for the *Catholic Biblical Quarterly*. Fitzmyer was editor from 1980 to 1984. Fitzmyer could not endure the shoddy scholarship and worse that hang around the fringes of biblical studies. He exposed the mistakes that he and other scholars found in the volume of the Dead Sea Scrolls edited by John Allegro.[54] Unlike many others, Fitzmyer from the outset suspected that the so-called Secret Gospel of Mark was a hoax (*America*, June 23, 1973).

Gustave Weigel, SJ (1906–64), after his doctorate at the Gregorian University on Faustus of Riez (1937), might have dedicated his research to the fathers of the Church. Instead, he enjoyed eleven happy years teaching theology at the Catholic University of Chile (Santiago), serving for six of those years as dean of the School of Theology. In 1948 he returned to the United States and spent the rest of his career teaching ecclesiology (the theological study of the Church) at Woodstock College. He was quickly involved in the ecumenical movement and was invited to lecture at leading universities, which included Brown, Harvard, Ohio State, Rutgers, Stanford, Vanderbilt, and Yale. He wrote *A Catholic Primer on the Ecumenical Movement*, the first number of *The Woodstock Papers*.[55] In 1960 he coauthored *An American Dialogue* with Robert McAfee Brown (1920–2001) of Union Theological Seminary (New York).[56] That same year he gave the Taylor Lectures at Yale Divinity School, the first Roman Catholic priest to give such an endowed series at Yale. Apart from his dedication to the ecumenical movement, he constantly encouraged American Catholic colleges and universities to engage in serious scholarship (above all in theology) and urged Americans in general to look beyond the Rio Grande with a desire to learn and serve. It was an enormous tragedy that his advice did nothing to prevent or at least to mitigate U.S. interventions in such countries as Guatemala, San Salvador, and Chile. A truly international theologian, Weigel spoke English, French, German, and Spanish. In 1953, he lectured at three German universities: Freiburg im Breisgau, Mainz, and Tübingen. Appointed one of the five North American consultors to the Secretariat for the Promotion of the Unity of Christians, Weigel attended the first two sessions of the Second Vatican Council and died of a coronary thrombosis before the third session began.[57]

Weigel's close associate, John Courtney Murray, was the only American Jesuit to be appointed an official *peritus* or expert at Vatican II. That contrasted with there being seven Italian Jesuit *periti* at the Council; two of them, Paolo Dezza[58] and Roberto Tucci, were future cardinals. *America* magazine warmly welcomed the calling of the Council by John XXIII and followed its proceedings assiduously. The magazine registered its satisfaction at Paul VI's inviting Murray to join him in concelebrating the Eucharist (*America*, September 2, 1967). It was the pope's way of thanking Murray for his central role in drafting the Declaration on Religious Liberty, *Dignitatis Humanae* (Of Human Dignity), finally promulgated on December 7, 1965.

During the four years of Vatican II and beyond, the American Jesuit journalist Daniel O'Hanlon did much to convey and recommend to a wide readership the achievements of the Council. As soon as Vatican II concluded, another American Jesuit, Walter M. Abbott (1923–2008), published *The Documents of Vatican II*, a still valuable translation with notes and comments by Catholic (eleven out of sixteen commentators were American Jesuits), Orthodox, and Protestant theologians, some of whom had been official observers. Selling more than a million copies, Abbott's volume symbolized how American Jesuits did much to interpret and implement the teaching of Vatican II, even if, apart from Murray (and unlike their fellow Jesuits from Austria, France, Germany, Holland, and Italy), they were not greatly involved in preparing the conciliar documents.

In the immediate aftermath of the Council, the Society of Jesus in the United States signaled its ecumenical commitment by moving its theologates from what John Havens Richards had called "remote" settings (see above) to share facilities and teaching with Episcopalians, Protestants, and Jews. In 1968, Weston School of Theology joined the Boston Theological Institute, a union of eight schools of theology, and shifted from the town of Weston to Cambridge, Massachusetts. There it shared a library and other buildings with Episcopal Theological School (also a member of the BTI), which was within a short walking distance from Harvard's Widener Library and the Harvard Divinity School (also a member of the BTI). Students enrolled in a school in the BTI could cross-register for courses or seminars in other schools. Some of the senior Jesuits on the faculty of Weston were worried that "the scholastics will rush off and take courses with Protestants." In fact, the number of students from other schools who enrolled for courses at

Weston exceeded the number of Jesuit scholastics enrolling for courses elsewhere.[59] Eventually falling numbers, rising costs, and other reasons led Weston Jesuit School of Theology in June 2008 to shift to Brighton, Massachusetts, affiliate with Boston College, and become Boston College School of Theology and Ministry.

On the West Coast, the Jesuit theologate south of San Francisco, Alma College, had moved in 1969 from its "remote" setting to an ecumenical consortium, the Graduate Theological Union in Berkeley. In 2009, while remaining in Berkeley and still a member college of the GTU, it became the Jesuit School of Theology of Santa Clara University.

In 1969 Woodstock College had also shifted from its rural setting to New York City and collaboration with Union Theological Seminary and the Jewish Theological Seminary. Woodstock closed in 1974 and was succeeded until 2013 by a research institute, Woodstock Theological Center, situated at Georgetown University. An extensive theological and philosophical library, which included some books that in 1869 had been taken out to Woodstock, Maryland, returned to the campus of Georgetown in 1975. The Woodstock library is still housed in the library at Georgetown University and retains its independence.

As carried forward by major theological institutions, Jesuit theology in the United States continues in two institutions on the East and the West Coast, respectively: Boston College School of Theology and Ministry and Jesuit School of Theology of Santa Clara University.

CHAPTER 2

PHILOSOPHICAL STUDIES AND AMERICAN JESUITS

FOR YEARS, ONE OF US (O'Collins) shared in the work of the Institute for Continuing Theological Education, offered under the auspices of the North American College (Rome) to American priests and some others. This course began with some successful lectures on philosophy by an Irish Dominican who taught at the Angelicum in Rome, Ambrose McNicholl. He opened the participants up to what followed when others presented developments in biblical studies, systematic theology, moral theology, and the rest. For many participants it was a startling and fruitful experience of how philosophy can lead into theological learning and updating.

In the United States most Jesuit scholastics (or students in training) followed the same order: first philosophy and then theology. But this was by no means the invariable sequence chosen by Jesuits for themselves or others. At Georgetown University, for instance, from 1817 philosophy was for many years considered the crowning course of the whole curriculum. From around 1900 to around 1960, neo-Scholastic philosophy, often understood as an equivalent for Thomism, continued to serve this purpose.[1] But with the Second Vatican Council (1962–65), the university dismantled the philosophical requirements, reducing them to two three-credit courses. Philosophy lost its cultural role as the force that could integrate the studies already done.[2]

We will see in the next chapter how Avery Dulles, SJ (1918–2008), published several influential books: notably, *Models of the*

Church (1974) and *Models of Revelation* (1983). These books showed Dulles in dialogue with a philosopher of religion, Ian Ramsey (1915–72). Ramsey, who had been a professor at the University of Oxford before being appointed bishop of Durham in 1966, wrote extensively on issues concerned with religious language or what he called "God-talk." When attempting to articulate something of the "mystery" of God, theologians can use "disclosure models." Ramsey's philosophical terminology of "mystery and models" proved valuable for Dulles in both books, especially in *Models of Revelation.*

Another philosophical influence showed up in *Models of Revelation*—not surprisingly, since questions about the divine self-revelation and our knowledge of God form the heart of fundamental theology, a discipline that draws heavily on philosophy and will be explained in the next chapter. A Hungarian polymath and brilliant scientist, Michael Polanyi (1891–1976), arrived at the University of Manchester in 1933 and turned philosopher to publish *Personal Knowledge* in 1958. Setting his face against mechanistic views of the world, Polanyi argued for the personal dimension of all knowledge, scientific, religious, and otherwise. A friend of Alan Turing (1912–54), who was highly influential in developing computer science and in breaking the German "Enigma" code during World War II, Polanyi was the teacher of two Nobel laureates and the father of another Nobel laureate. His epistemology or theory of knowledge proved its worth for the theology of Dulles.

Unquestionably other philosophical studies (from Plato and Aristotle to modern authors) prepared and shaped the theological mind of Dulles, right from his undergraduate studies at Harvard University and hence years before he became a Jesuit and studied theology. His dialogue with the thought of Ramsey and Polanyi yields a vignette of how philosophy continued to affect his theological thinking and writing.

The Second Vatican Council underlined the importance of philosophical studies but declined to single out Thomism as deserving preeminence in Catholic philosophy or theology (*Optatam Totius* 15). Pope John Paul II, in his 1998 encyclical *Fides et Ratio* (On the Relationship between Faith and Reason), delineated at length the indispensable role of philosophical reason for theological faith, the interaction between theology and philosophy, and what Christian believers should expect from the particular philosophies they choose to study.[3]

All theology will remain low on clarity and substance unless it puts the Scriptures and history/tradition into dialogue with philosophy. From the time of Justin Martyr in the second century, philosophical views of God, the created world, and the divine interaction with the world have assisted the interpretation and appropriation of the biblical witness. In general, philosophical reason sharpens the questions to be asked and the methods to be followed, throws light on human beings and their world, and brings conceptual clarity to bear on biblical texts, which by and large are prephilosophical. It also illuminates what happens when we read and interpret the Scriptures. By developing insights into the nature of knowledge, meaning, truth, and hermeneutics, philosophy can elucidate to a degree the spiritual dynamism operating when we read, hear, and pray over the Scriptures.[4]

FROM ST. IGNATIUS TO WORLD WAR II

Not surprisingly, the Jesuit *Constitutions* written by St. Ignatius Loyola (1491–1556) proposed the study of the philosophy of Aristotle, with special esteem paid to his successor, St. Thomas Aquinas (iv.5).[5] Yet the Fifth General Congregation of Jesuits in 1593 allowed for a certain flexibility: "It is not fitting that Ours be more tightly bound to St. Thomas than are the Thomists themselves." By that time, Francisco Suárez (1548–1617) was emerging as the most influential Jesuit Thomist.

The innovative and sometimes contested views of Suárez divided Jesuits into different camps.[6] He studied and wrote at a time of renewed enthusiasm for Aquinas, who had been named a doctor of the Church in 1567. While shaped by the philosophical thought of Aquinas and highly respectful of him, Suárez did not hesitate to disagree on such issues as (a) "the distinction between essence and existence, which he [Suárez] considered to be only a mental distinction in finite beings, and [b] the principle of individuation, which he believed was found in the *entitas* of a thing and not in designated matter."[7]

In an age when rulers were becoming absolutist and asserting monarchy by divine right, Suárez in *Defensio Fidei* not only justified popular revolt but also criticized the requirement of James I that his "Catholic subjects take an oath of fidelity."[8] For Suárez political authority belonged to the people. He provided a philosophical basis for the democratic government that would come in the United States.

After the Society of Jesus was fully restored in 1814, Suárezian thought returned, but only for a time. Pope Leo XIII prescribed, in his 1879 encyclical *Aeterni Patris* (Of the Eternal Father), that Catholic faculties teach Thomism.[9] As we noted in chapter 1, an enthusiastic follower of Suárez taught on the theology faculty at the very start of Woodstock College (1869), but the influence of Suárez in the United States and elsewhere gradually fell away. His open-mindedness was alien to some nineteenth-century Jesuit philosophy, which "became apologetics for a Church which felt threatened by the age and its scientific advances. Debates gave way to uniformity and ideological correctness."[10] In Rome, the French Jesuit Louis Billot (1846–1931) caused "the entire philosophical doctrine and a great part of the theological theses of Suárez and Molina [of whom more below] to disappear from the Gregorian University." At the time of the Modernist controversy, Billot claimed that the Modernists "only have to open Suárez and they will find there all their teaching."[11]

The 1917 Code of Canon Law encouraged sidelining Suárez by proposing Aquinas as teacher of philosophy and theology in Catholic seminaries (canons 589 and 1366). Nevertheless, Włodzimierz Ledóchowski (1866–1942), the Jesuit general (1916–42), in a forty-page letter, "On Following the Doctrine of St Thomas," while reiterating the rejection of Kant and Modernism, promoted study of Suárez. "He quoted the Dominican cardinal and Thomistic scholar Zephyrinus Gonzales (1831–1889), who asserted that Suárez, after Thomas himself, was the most outstanding representative of Scholastic philosophy, and that his ideas explain, weigh, and develop Aquinas's views 'with extraordinary clarity.'" Ledóchowski also claimed, "Pope Benedict XV's blessing for saying that Jesuits were quite entitled to hold their traditional views of disputed points in Aquinas, among which was the denial of the real distinction between essence and existence."[12]

In the event, many Jesuits sided with Thomism, while some remained Suárezians. Cyril A. Vollert, SJ (1901–80), of St. Mary's College, Kansas, encouraged both sides. He translated into English works by both Aquinas and Suárez.

After World War I, the French philosophers Étienne Gilson (1884–1978) and Jacques Maritain (1882–1973) lectured in North

America as well as in France and elsewhere in Europe. Their interpretation of St. Thomas and the so-called *philosophia perennis* had some impact on American Catholic philosophers—in particular, the Jesuits at Fordham and Saint Louis University. Other French philosophers also enjoyed an influence in North America: for example, Henri Bergson (1859–1941) and Maurice Blondel (1861–1949).[13] Gabriel Marcel (1889–1976) spread his form of existentialism by lecturing and publishing in the United States and Canada. Let us speak briefly of Maritain and Marcel.

From the 1930s, French, German, Italian, and other European scientists and intellectuals found a new home on American campuses. One of these was Maritain, already acclaimed among the great thinkers of the century. In 1940, he sat down with Robert I. Gannon, the president of Fordham University, to discuss his coming to Fordham as chair of the graduate philosophy program. Raymond Schroth tells the story: "Maritain was opposed to the relationship between the Vatican and the Mussolini fascist government. He wanted assurance from Gannon that he could speak out on political issues that were not governed by the content of revelation. Gannon, a pro-Franco conservative, refused." Maritain left to lecture at a dozen other universities until 1960, finishing at Princeton.[14]

In 1961–62, Marcel gave the William James Lectures at Harvard University. He had already visited Gonzaga University, Spokane, Washington, to lecture in 1960 and enjoyed a "tremendous reception" (the Town and Gown Forum of Gonzaga University). In April 1963, he was back at Gonzaga to speak on "the Responsibility of the Philosopher in the Contemporary World." The message of Marcel emerged from a noble and personal view of human beings. "Man [*sic*] is not a mere problem, an object which can be systematically defined in terms of facts and functions. Man is a mystery and can be truly defined only in an existential situation by his participation in the world around him."

Two months later, in June 1963, another notable philosopher, this time a Jesuit, Martin D'Arcy of Campion Hall, Oxford University, came to Gonzaga via Georgetown, Boston College, and Fordham and spoke about "some Problems of the Self." Marcel would have preferred "the Mystery of the Self."

FROM WORLD WAR II TO POPE JOHN PAUL II

A generation of Jesuit philosophical giants emerged in the aftermath of the Second World War. They included Bernard J. Lonergan (1904–84), Walter J. Ong (1912–2003), W. Norris Clarke (1915–2008), and Patrick Aidan Heelan (1926–2015). Boston, St. Louis, New York, and Georgetown were major scenes for their activity.

(1) After finishing his doctorate at the Gregorian University in 1940 (on Aquinas's understanding of divine grace and human freedom), Lonergan began in Montreal a forty-three-year career of writing and teaching (that took him to Regis College [Toronto], the Gregorian University, Harvard University, and Boston College).[15] His contribution to the work of American Jesuits began quickly. In the newly founded *Theological Studies*, he published his doctorate in four parts (1941–42). His now famous "Verbum" articles appeared in the same quarterly (1946–49) and elucidated Aquinas's theory of knowledge. After he began teaching at the Gregorian in 1953, where he enjoyed instructing numerous American students, he published (in 1957) *Insight*, the study of human understanding that made him famous around the world.

A notable *peritus* or official consultant at Vatican II, Lonergan was appointed a member of the first International Theological Commission. Lung cancer led him to leave the Gregorian in 1965 and return to Canada. He continued to engage himself with philosophy and theology (in particular, questions of fundamental theology). His *Method in Theology* (1972) has proved enduringly influential, as have his views on cognitional theory and human consciousness. Our next chapter will provide further details of his achievements from 1965 until his death in late 1984—achievements that deeply affected, among other things, Jesuit philosophical studies in the United States.

(2) Saint Louis University's School of Philosophy and Letters was founded in 1889 and developed the tradition of "Missouri Valley Thomism."[16] In 1925, two Saint Louis Jesuit

scholastics established a journal to promote neo-Scholastic philosophy, *The Modern Schoolman*. One of the oldest philosophical journals in North America, in 2013 it was renamed *Res Philosophica*. After World War II, such notable Jesuit professors as Robert J. Henle (1909–2000) and George P. Klubertanz (1912–72) furthered the renewal of Thomist studies at SLU. Garth L. Hallett, SJ (b. 1927), who served as dean of Philosophy and Letters (1985–2009), brought different approaches and emphases. His philosophical mind was shaped by analytic philosophy and the thought of Ludwig Wittgenstein, as one sees in his *Wittgenstein's Definition of Meaning as Use* (1967) and *A Companion to Wittgenstein's "Philosophical Investigations"* (1977). Hallett's creativity has continued into his nineties; witness his *The Maturing of Monotheism: A Dialectical Path to Its Truth* (2019). A non-Jesuit, Leonard James Eslick (1914–91), also took his students beyond Thomism by introducing them to process philosophy. In *The Modern Schoolman* and other journals, he published numerous articles on the thought of those who founded process philosophy, Alfred North Whitehead and Charles Hartshorne. Eslick taught at SLU from 1948 until his death in 1991.

But it was another non-Jesuit professor, James D. Collins (1917–85), who proved larger than life. Acclaimed a giant at SLU for his studies in ancient, medieval, and modern philosophy, he was the doyen of Missouri Valley Thomism. Collins did not restrict himself to that school of philosophy, publishing significant works, for instance, on European existentialist and rationalist philosophy. He taught at SLU from 1945 until his death.

A very significant Jesuit professor at SLU, who ranged even further beyond the Thomist tradition, can be described as "a personalist philosopher of culture."[17] Walter Ong explored the structure of our knowing and the implications of the development from oral culture to print culture, where knowledge became "mapped." During the 1930s and 1940s, he remained in dialogue with the Canadian communications theorist, Marshall McLuhan. A visiting professor at several prestigious American universities, Ong lectured around the world, and at home in the United States he was honored by being elected president of the powerful Modern Language Association (1978).

(3) After earning his doctorate at Louvain, "Norrie" Clarke spent his life teaching at Fordham University. Étienne Gilson's exposition of Aquinas helped shape Clarke's starting point. He also drew from (a) Joseph Maréchal, SJ (1878–1944), who confronted Thomism with the critical philosophy of Immanuel Kant, and from (b) contemporary currents of personalism and phenomenology, especially the work of Martin Buber.

Clarke understood philosophy to be "the critically reflective, systematically articulated attempt to illumine our human experience in depth and set it in a vision of the whole" (*The One and the Many: A Contemporary Thomistic Metaphysics*, 2001). Here he noted how a "good metaphysician needed both a diving suit and a set of wings—the diving suit to explore the particulars of reality with as much detail and depth as needed and the wings to soar as high as needed to be able to see how everything adds up." Reference to "the wings," consciously or unconsciously, recalled his experience as a young teenager when he took a risky jump from one ledge on a cliff to another and enjoyed his "first intuition of being."

Clarke's creative retrieval of Aquinas involved integrating Thomistic metaphysics with personalism.[18] He inserted into Thomism modern insights about (a) the human person and (b) the relational dimension of all being or "substance in relation." This meant that Clarke strongly identified with the personalist Thomism of St. John Paul II (pope 1978–2005) and drew the comment that this personalism could lead to "waves of sex."[19]

It is hard to exaggerate the wide influence of Clarke as a philosopher, priest, and teacher on generation after generation of Fordham students. He was the cofounder and editor (1961–85) of the *International Philosophical Quarterly*. The author or coauthor of over sixty books, he was awarded the Aquinas Medal in 1980 by the American Catholic Philosophical Association. The first two recipients of this medal were Maritain (1951) and Gilson (1952). Other recipients have been Lonergan (1970), Frederick C. Copleston, SJ (1977), and Quentin Lauer, SJ (1985).

During his many years at Fordham, Clarke enjoyed working with several distinguished Jesuit philosophical colleagues. William J. R. Richardson (1920–2016) taught there before moving in 1981 to Boston College. The phenomenology of Martin Heidegger (1889–1976), while enjoying considerable influence in philosophy and theology in Europe, was sometimes dismissed in the United States as merely belonging to the history of literature. Richardson remedied this situation by producing the first comprehensive study of Heidegger; he also wrote the entry "Heidegger, Martin" for D. M. Borchert (ed.), *The Encyclopedia of Philosophy, Supplement.*[20] Richardson helped to dispel the monopoly of analytic philosophy that had characterized schools of philosophy in North America and elsewhere in the English-speaking world.

Quentin Lauer, SJ (1917–97), studied in Paris and wrote a doctorate for the Sorbonne on Edmund Husserl (1859–1938), a key figure at the origins of modern phenomenology. Lauer became a major player in introducing into the United States phenomenology, as well as the thought of Georg Wilhelm Friedrich Hegel (1770–1831). Professor at Fordham from 1954 to 1994, in the mid-1960s Lauer engaged in dialogue with Marxism and, in particular, with the French Communist Roger Garaudy; they wrote together *A Christian-Communist Dialogue* (1968). Lauer devoted the rest of his career to studying and expounding Hegel.

Clarke enjoyed for a time working with another important colleague in the person of the Irish American Patrick Aidan Heelan (1926–2015), a notable Jesuit philosopher of science. During his studies for a MA in Dublin (at University College, Dublin), Heelan worked at the Dublin Institute of Advanced Studies with Erwin Schrödiner and John Synge, mathematicians famous for their contributions to general relativity and cosmology. He took his (first) doctorate at the Institute of Geophysics of Saint Louis University, concentrating on the philosophy of modern physics from the phenomenological and hermeneutical perspective of Husserl and Heidegger. He went on to complete a second doctorate (1964) at the Catholic University of Louvain (Belgium), studying logic and Husserlian philosophy and initiating contacts with Werner Heisenberg (at the Max Planck Institute for Physics and Astrophysics in Munich)—contacts maintained until the death of Heisenberg in 1976. Heelan's second doctoral dissertation, *Quantum Mechanics and Objectivity* (1965), put him at the forefront of the philosophy of science.

Heelan taught at Fordham University and the State University of New York at Stony Brook, before becoming the William A. Gaston Professor of Philosophy at Georgetown University (1995–2013). He has been among the most distinguished Jesuit philosophers of science in American history. He is remembered not only for numerous articles but also for such books as *Space Perception and the Philosophy of Science* (1983) and his posthumous *The Observable—Heisenberg's Philosophy of Quantum Mechanics* (2016).

When recalling the Jesuit philosophers who taught alongside Clarke, one should not neglect Robert O. Johann (1924–2009). At Fordham University he began teaching as a Jesuit, left the Society of Jesus, and returned after a year to resume teaching at Fordham. He specialized in research and writing on the philosophy of love, continuing the path he chose for his early books: *The Meaning of Love: An Essay Towards a Metaphysics of Intersubjectivity* (1955) and *The Primacy of Love* (1959).

COPLESTON, MOLINA, AND THE GREGORIAN

Frederick Copleston (1907–94) rightly deserved his place in the *Cambridge Encyclopedia of Jesuits*. This erudite English convert to Catholicism taught philosophy at Heythrop College, Oxfordshire, for thirty years, serving also as visiting professor for the Gregorian University during the first semester from 1952 to 1968. Dissatisfied with current histories of philosophy, Copleston wrote a monumental nine-volume history of Western philosophy that was published between 1946 and 1975. It brought him worldwide acclaim. In Rome and, occasionally, at Heythrop College, Copleston taught philosophy to American students. As a visiting professor he twice taught at Santa Clara University, California. His masterpiece, *A History of Philosophy*, is found in Jesuit libraries in the United States and around the world.[21]

From 1953 to 1965, Copleston shared the same Jesuit community (the Gregorian) with Lonergan. The only written comment we have found by Copleston on Lonergan comes in a footnote: "The writings of Lonergan, the Canadian Thomist, seem to be free of Heideggerian influence."[22] But why did Copleston expect such an influence? Robert Doran, SJ, in a private communication, told us that Lonergan "spoke very warmly about Fr. Copleston on several occasions in conversations that we had." Doran drew our attention to Lonergan citing Copleston appreciatively not only in *Method in Theology* but also in volumes 13, 17, and 18 of *The Collected Works of Bernard Lonergan*.

During his lifetime Copleston made his major contribution to philosophy in the United States. It was long after his death that the Spanish Jesuit Luis de Molina (1535–1600) aroused vigorous debate in the United States. Molina's *scientia media* ("middle knowledge"), a theory about free will, aimed at reconciling human freedom with the divine foreknowledge of everything that will happen. Molina suggested that God knows and takes into account decisions that rational creatures would freely make in any situation in which they might be placed. Molina called it "middle" knowledge, because it is more than a knowledge of mere possibilities but less than a vision of actual future events. God gives the grace, arranges circumstances to bring about the proper result, and foresees our future actions. Since the divine foresight "depends" on our free decisions, Molina called it *scientia conditionata*, or knowledge relative to future human decisions and actions.[23] Since the 1970s, Alvin Plantinga (b. 1932) and other philosophers have revived interest in and stirred up fresh debate about Molina's theory. It was Plantinga (a Protestant philosopher) and his colleagues, rather than any American Jesuits, who launched a renewed debate about Molinism.[24]

A cohort of American Jesuits have continued to carry philosophy forward: for instance, Harry J. Gensler (b. 1945) and Thomas J. Regan (b. 1954) in Chicago; William R. Rehg (b. 1952) at Saint Louis University; Arthur R. Madigan (b. 1946) at Boston College; Joseph W. Koterski (b. 1953) at Fordham University; and John J. Conley (b. 1951) at Loyola University Maryland in Baltimore. Koterski is the current editor of the *International Philosophical Quarterly*, the journal founded by Clarke (see above). Koterski coedited with Conley two books on the teaching of Pope John Paul II (including one on his ethical doctrine), while Conley himself has done groundbreaking work on French women who contributed to the philosophical debates of the early modern period but who have been ignored in standard histories of philosophy. His *Suspicion of Virtue: Women Philosophers in Neoclassical France* (Cornell University Press, 2002) sets the record straight.

When detailing Jesuit philosophical influence in the United States, we may not ignore the offshore influence (on American students and American philosophy) exercised through the Gregorian University. We mentioned above Lonergan's twelve years at the Gregorian and the seventeen semesters Copleston spent teaching philosophy there. We should not forget the American Jesuits who have belonged to the Gregorian's philosophy faculty. With a DPhil on Aristotle from the University of Oxford, Kevin L. Flannery (b. 1950) still teaches at the Gregorian, where he was dean of Faculty of Philosophy (1999–2005). Catholic University of America Press published in 2013 his *Action and Character According to Aristotle: The Logic of the Moral Life.* A Maltese-American, Louis Caruana, joined the philosophy faculty at the Gregorian (1995), took his PhD in the philosophy of science at the University of Cambridge (1997), and did research at the University of Notre Dame, Indiana (2009). He has specialized in lecturing and publications on Galileo, Darwin, and many philosophical themes raised by modern science. In 2014 he was appointed dean of the Gregorian's Faculty of Philosophy. In the best Jesuit tradition, Caruana speaks numerous languages and has lectured in Brazil, India, Vietnam, Africa, Australia, and across Europe.

Before ending this stock-taking of Jesuit contributions to the American philosophical scene, we would be remiss if we failed to mention philosophical ethics. Other chapters (chaps. 1 and 4) have much to add about questions of moral theology (e.g., social issues) and what Jesuits contributed. The frontier between moral theology and philosophical ethics remains porous.

CONCLUSION

While neither of us have ever taught for a school of philosophy, our contacts with Jesuit philosophers in the United States and elsewhere have been extensive. We conclude with the account of a dramatic encounter (between O'Collins and a Jesuit philosopher) in the fall of 1970:

A group of Jesuit philosophers had invited me as an interested theologian to Saint Louis for the annual meeting of their North American Council on Belief and Unbelief—the most dramatic conference I have ever attended. In the fall of 1970 I joined Edward MacKinnon, a Jesuit friend and philosopher from Boston College, for the flight out and back from Boston to Saint Louis. In 1969 he had agreed to prepare the main position paper for the next meeting. In the course of the year he ceased to believe in God. His paper movingly put the case for his own unbelief. Ed's announcement startled and saddened the other Jesuits, but no one tried to wheedle, let alone bully, him back into belief. Nevertheless, many of us challenged the way Ed decided the issue of belief and unbelief in terms of the internal logic of the arguments. To say the least, this approach bypassed the element of free decision that affects the whole life (and not merely the arguments) of anyone who asks: Does God exist?

On the flight back to Boston, a strong tailwind boosted the speed of our almost empty aircraft to seven hundred miles an hour—the fastest I have ever flown. Ed plied me with bourbon and asked: "Why do you believe in God?" All I could say was "God seems as real to me as someone sitting down the aisle from us." Ed left the Jesuit order, married, and taught philosophy for the University of California. I always remember his question, and still cannot truly answer it in any other way.

CHAPTER 3

THEOLOGY, PATRISTICS, AND CHURCH HISTORY

HAVING EXAMINED THE STORY of the Jesuit commitment to philosophy, we turn now to theology as such. First, we take up fundamental or foundational theology.

FUNDAMENTAL THEOLOGY

Fundamental theology is that branch of theology that studies such foundational issues as the divine revelation in the history of Israel and Jesus Christ, the conditions that open up human beings in faith to this self-communication of God, the signs that make faith in Christ a credible option, the transmission (through the Church's tradition and the inspired Scriptures) of the experience of divine self-communication, and the nature of theological method. The prehistory of fundamental theology stretches back to the second- and third-century apologists who rebutted objections and offered educated outsiders a case for Christian faith. After the Society of Jesus was founded in the sixteenth century, apologetic literature continued to take shape around three questions: the existence of God, the divine identity of Christ, and the establishment of the Church. In his "controversial theology" the Jesuit St. Robert Bellarmine (1542–1621) debated with Anglican and Protestant counterparts, including King James I of England and Scotland, basic issues concerning the third question, the Church founded by Christ.[1]

After their restoration in 1814 and through the nineteenth into the twentieth century, Jesuits in the United States began contributing to fundamental theology but mostly remained content to develop in a nonhistorical way the "triple demonstration," now practiced by neo-Scholastic authors. A Harvard graduate and Catholic convert who taught at Woodstock College (1960–74), Catholic University of America (1974–88), and Fordham University (1988–2008), Avery Dulles, SJ, eventually changed that.[2] His *Apologetics and the Biblical Christ* (1963) showed how reading the Gospels as religious testimony, which embraces both factual memories and spiritual insights, establishes the credibility of Christian faith in Jesus risen from the dead and truly divine. Dulles examined apologetics in the post–New Testament context with *A History of Apologetics* (1970). While recognizing the apologetical responsibilities of fundamental theologians, he did not wish to follow those who reduced fundamental theology to apologetics.

In *Survival of Dogma* (1971), Dulles, in the words of Patrick Carey, "reinterpreted Catholic notions of revelation and dogma in the developmental, interpersonal, and symbolic categories of theologians in the Transcendental [read Karl Rahner] and *nouvelle théologie* [read Yves Congar, Jean Daniélou, and Henri de Lubac] tradition of Vatican II."[3] Dulles continued to publish work on divine revelation and its human counterpart, faith. This culminated first in "what is perhaps his most significant contribution to fundamental theology, *Models of Revelation* (1983)."[4] Examining modern Protestant and Catholic notions of revelation, Dulles described five widely held models: revelation as propositional, historical, mystical, dialectical, and bringing new awareness. He developed his own model of revelation as symbolic mediation, a model that synthesizes the best features of the other five models. This understanding of revelation served to underpin much of what he developed on questions of apologetics, catechesis, ecumenism, and evangelization.

Logically, his exploration of revelation led Dulles to write a theology of the human response to divine revelation in Christian faith, *The Assurance of Things Hoped For* (1994), and a more popular version for a general reading public, *The New World of Faith* (2000). *The Assurance*, while not enjoying the widespread impact of *Models of Revelation*, seems to have been the first major, modern work on faith published in English by a Catholic theologian. His work in fundamental theology and in ecclesiology (see below) led Dulles to be appointed to important commissions (e.g., the Lutheran-Catholic dialogue [1971–96]) and to become an expert for the United States Conference of Catholic Bishops (USCCB) in preparing the *Catechism of the Catholic Church* (1992).

When assessing the scope of Jesuit influence on fundamental theology in the United States, one should recall further individuals. Michael J. Buckley, SJ (1931–2019), provided outstanding studies in the foundational area of belief and nonbelief: *At the Origins of Modern Atheism* (1987) and *Denying and Disclosing God: The Continuing Progress of Modern Atheism* (2004). These works, both published by Yale University Press, established Buckley as a world authority in this area. His worth was recognized in his appointment as a consultant to the USCCB on doctrine.

Let us also cite examples of significant conferences in the area of fundamental theology. These meetings proved successful and influential for this sector of theology.

Over the weekend of October 8–10, 1971, Woodstock College, along with the American Teilhard de Chardin Association, Trinity Institute, and Union Theological College, sponsored a conference in New York City on hope and the future of humanity. More than eight hundred professors of theology, seminarians, and other interested people attended and heard lectures from representatives of three currents of thought: the theologians of hope, process theologians, and the followers of Pierre Teilhard de Chardin. Christopher Mooney, president of Woodstock College now located during its final years of existence in New York (1969–74), spoke for Teilhard's evolutionary optimism. Jürgen Moltmann (b. 1926), made famous by his *Theology of Hope* (German original 1964), flew in from Tübingen to present one of the main papers. He pointed out that the invited participants included no women, no poor people, no one from the third world, and only one black theologian, his friend James Cone (1938–2018).[5]

In September 1987, on the occasion of the tercentenary of the publication by Sir Isaac Newton (1642–1727) of *Philosophiae Naturalis Principia Mathematica*, Jesuit astronomers and other specialists, led by George V. Coyne (1933–2020), the American director of the Vatican Observatory at Castel Gandolfo, held a study week on the relationship between theology, philosophy, and the natural sciences. Even before the twenty-one distinguished participants, who included the American Jesuits Michael J. Buckley and Richard J. Clifford (see chap. 5 below), met, Pope John Paul II wrote to Coyne. The pope went into detail about the dialogue to be promoted between theology and science for the good of both.[6]

Jesuit astronomers, such as Americans William Stoeger (1943–2014)[7] and Guy Consolmagno (b. 1952), continued to promote that healthy dialogue between faith and science which belongs to fundamental theology. They did so through meetings at Castel Gandolfo, joint work with the University of Arizona, various meetings, and publications. The Jesuits of the Vatican Observatory responded, for instance, to questions raised by John Paul II by bringing together scientists, theologians, and other experts, both Catholics and other Christians, to explore, in the light of the laws of nature, belief in the bodily resurrection. An American Jesuit, Brian Daley, SJ (see below), contributed a paper on early Christian ways of articulating faith in the resurrection.[8]

Consolmagno has excelled at sharing theological questions raised by discoveries of astronomers. In *America* magazine he greeted the first photograph of a black hole by asking: "Can You Find God in a Black Hole?" (April 10, 2019).

At Easter 1996, two Jesuits, one American (Dan Kendall) and one Australian (Gerald O'Collins), joined forces with a Presbyterian friend (Professor Stephen Davis of Claremont, California) to run the first of four "summits" in New York City: an international, ecumenical, interdisciplinary symposium on the resurrection of Jesus Christ. *Newsweek* turned the symposium and its subject into its cover story, and major TV networks gave the "resurrection summit" generous attention. Oxford University Press published the proceedings, *The Resurrection* (1997), and did so for three subsequent "summits" (see below). In a TV interview, Davis summed up the common faith of the symposiasts: "Unless Jesus rose from the dead, none of us have any hope."

Several of the scholars who participated in that resurrection symposium came from Europe and Australia—a reminder that the Jesuits and others who have played their part in shaping theology in the United States have also come from elsewhere. They have done so through teaching, publishing, and collaboration with American associates.

The crowning work of the Jesuit theologian Karl Rahner (1904–84), *Foundations of Christian Faith* (German original 1976), drew together his response to fundamental issues with which he grappled over a lifetime: What is Christian faith? How can one justify it and live it with intellectual honesty? Does faith cohere with the basic dynamism of the human spirit? Rahner's classic volume remains a holistic *apologia* for God's answer to the universal questions of human beings. It uses contemporary human understanding and his own experience of the Spiritual Exercises of St. Ignatius Loyola to validate the divine self-communication in Christ and the Church founded by him. When René Latourelle and Gerald O'Collins edited a book that aimed to map the identity of fundamental theology, *Problems and Perspectives of Fundamental Theology* (Italian original, 1980), Rahner contributed a chapter, "Observations on the Situation of Faith Today." Marked by Ignatian spirituality, he left aside any limited attempt to provide merely rational grounds for faith and incorporated something of the decision-making process provided by the Spiritual Exercises.[9]

Rahner visited the United States to lecture and found a ready audience. American Jesuits, especially those who had studied with him in Germany, like William V. Dych (1932–2000), Leo J. O'Donovan (b. 1934), and Harvey D. Egan (b. 1937), expounded and spread in the United States his theology and, in particular, his fundamental theology.[10] Dych, who had done his doctoral research with Rahner at the Universities of Munich and Münster, acted as Rahner's interpreter on his American tours and prepared the English translation of *Foundations of Christian Faith*. This volume enjoyed special authority at the University of Notre Dame, Indiana, and in other important theological centers across the United States. Fordham University has a Karl Rahner Professor of Theology. Gerald A. McCool, SJ, spread Rahner's ideas through his teaching at Fordham and through such books as the *Theology of Karl Rahner* (1961) and a *Rahner Reader* (1975).

Rightly dissatisfied with early twentieth-century fundamental theology and its philosophical underpinnings, the Canadian Bernard Lonergan, SJ, an exact contemporary of Rahner, developed, as we noted in the last chapter, his own philosophical prolegomena to theology that he hoped would be useful for other disciplines: *Insight: A Study of Human Understanding* (1957). Subsequently in *Method in Theology* (1972), mirroring the change from classicist to modern culture, he set out what he called a "fifth functional specialty, foundations." It followed four other specialties (research, interpretation, history, and dialectic) and presented the horizon within which the meaning of doctrines can be apprehended. His foundations elucidate conflicts revealed in dialectic, and provide guidance for the remaining specialties, concerned, respectively, with doctrines, systematics, and communications. In 1971–72, Lonergan was the Stillman Professor of Roman Catholic Theological Studies at Harvard University. For eight years from 1975, as Visiting Distinguished Professor at Boston College, he taught seminars, tutored students, and discussed his theological and philosophical ideas with faculty. Thanks to Robert M. Doran, SJ, and other Jesuits (and non-Jesuits), Lonergan's ideas spread across the United States and around the world and enriched Christian theology and, specifically, fundamental theology.[11]

Gerald O'Collins often lectured in the United States: at Weston School of Theology (1968–72) a semester each year; in summer schools (lasting for several weeks) or on other occasions—at Boston College, Fairfield University, Georgetown University, Gonzaga University, the Josephinum (Columbus, OH), Providence College, Sacred Heart University (Fairfield, CT), Saint Louis University, Saint Michael's College (Burlington, VT), Seattle University, Seton Hall University, Trinity College (Burlington, VT), University of Chicago Divinity School, University of Dallas, University of Notre Dame (often), the University of San Francisco (often), the University of Wisconsin at Madison, and Yale; and at Marquette University for three semesters as Francis Wade Professor (1994, 1998, and 2006). His years in Rome (1973–2006) involved teaching well over a thousand American seminarians and young priests who came to Rome to live at the North American College (or elsewhere) and study for degrees in theology. He also lectured year after year to American priests who attended programs in continuing theological education. On several occasions groups of American bishops visited Rome for updating courses. They brought with them speakers from the United States, like Raymond Brown, but mainly used professors who held chairs in the ecclesiastical universities of the eternal city.[12] O'Collins was called on to lecture not only in Christology but also in fundamental theology, a field in which he has published frequently: for instance, *Foundations of Theology* (1971), *Fundamental Theology* (1981), *Jesus Risen* (1981), *Rethinking Fundamental Theology* (2011), *Believing in the Resurrection* (2012), and the trilogy—*Revelation* (2016), *Inspiration* (2018), and *Tradition* (2018). Both in the United States and through activity in Rome, O'Collins contributed to American fundamental theology, using human experience and hope as keys toward understanding the foundational human contact with God through Jesus Christ and his Holy Spirit.

Considered by many the doyen of modern fundamental theology, a Canadian Jesuit, René Latourelle (1918–2017) spent his life teaching at the Gregorian University. Set on reforming studies in the light of Vatican II, for twelve years he served as dean of the theology faculty.[13] He added to his notable influence on American theology by coediting the 1,264-page *The Dictionary of Fundamental Theology* (*DFT*; New York: Crossroad, 1994). Forty Jesuits contributed to this basic reference work on fundamental theology, the only one of its kind in modern times. They included the Americans Avery Dulles, John O'Donnell, Francis Sullivan, and Jared Wicks. Four American provinces of the Society of Jesus, along with four other Jesuit provinces, helped cover the costs of translation and publication.

The *DFT* attended to a former Jesuit, Hans Urs von Balthasar (1905–88), by including two articles on him by Rino (later Archbishop) Fisichella. In twentieth-century fundamental theology, von Balthasar proved very significant by rehabilitating beauty over against meaning/truth and goodness. It is through beauty that we come to truth and goodness. Regrettably, von Balthasar declined to be a visiting professor at the Gregorian. Nevertheless, Fisichella, Latourelle, and O'Donnell promoted research into his work among graduate students at the Gregorian. An American Jesuit, Joseph Fessio, did the theological public an enormous service through publishing in English fifteen volumes by von Balthasar (Ignatius Press, San Francisco).

CHRISTOLOGY AND TRINITY

In the areas of Christology and the doctrine of the Trinity, we should recall such American Jesuits as Michael Cook (*Christology as Narrative Quest*, 1993), Brian McDermott (*Word Become Flesh: Dimensions of Christology*, 1993), Roger Haight (*Jesus, Symbol of God*, 1999), and Thomas Rausch (*Who Is Jesus? An Introduction to Christology*, 2003). Each, in his own way, wanted to show how belief in Christ and the tripersonal God shapes living faith and does not remain a mere matter of verbal orthodoxy inherited from the early Church. An appendix to this chapter wittily exhibits this kind of "orthodoxy" that Jesuit students at Woodstock College and very often elsewhere learned by heart before facing the examinations.

The proceedings of the New York "summits," coedited by Davis, Kendall, and O'Collins and published by Oxford University Press, included volumes on Christ in himself (*The Incarnation*, 2002), on Christ for us (*The Redemption*, 2004), and on the Trinity (*The Trinity*, 1999)—all well reviewed and widely read. *The Redemption* prompted O'Collins's own study, also with Oxford University Press, *Jesus Our Redeemer* (2007), which interpreted Christ's redemption as liberation from evil, expiation of sin, and the work of love.

O'Collins also published, with Oxford University Press, *Christology* (1995; rev. ed. 2009), and, with Paulist Press, *The Tripersonal God* (1999; rev. ed. 2014). The former has sold up to forty thousand copies and the latter over twelve thousand copies. He anticipated and complemented these major works with a number of smaller books: for instance, the best-selling 1977 *What Are They Saying About Jesus?*, which inaugurated for Paulist Press the What Are They Saying About (WATSA) series, and *Incarnation* (Continuum, 2002), which was translated into Italian, Norwegian, and Spanish. The experience of the polyvalent *presence* of the risen Christ has shaped the Christology of O'Collins.

Many American Jesuits and their students have treasured an introduction to Christology, *Who Do You Say I Am?* (1994), authored by Jacques Dupuis, SJ (1923–2004), a Belgian who spent the last twenty years of his life at the Gregorian. *Jesus the Christ* (1976) by Walter (later Cardinal) Kasper, which also emerged from lectures at the Gregorian, was widely used by Jesuit colleges and universities in the United States. Kasper's *The God of Jesus Christ* (1989) proved a popular text for courses on the Trinity.

ECCLESIOLOGY

Two figures seize our attention when we enquire about Jesuits who in the United States have made notable contributions to the doctrine of the Church (ecclesiology): Avery Dulles and Francis A. Sullivan (1922–2019).[14] After Gustave Weigel died in 1964 (see chap. 1), Dulles began teaching the ecclesiology courses at Woodstock College. He had already been asked to be the Catholic commentator on Vatican II's Dogmatic Constitution on the Church, *Lumen Gentium* (the

Light of the Nations), for Walter Abbott's *The Documents of Vatican II*, which appeared at the end of 1965. Dulles then produced *The Dimensions of the Church* (1967), "a postconciliar reflection" that filled out how he understood Vatican II's vision of the Catholic Church.

Less than a decade later Dulles published his highly successful *Models of the Church* (1974; expanded and revised editions 1987 and 2002). Here he deployed to great advantage the scheme of "mystery and models," a scheme he was to use subsequently in his *Models of Revelation*. The mystery of the Church has been expressed through different models, and Dulles named five of them: the Church as institution, mystical communion, sacrament, herald, and servant. No single model captures the mystery of the Church, each of them discloses something, and we need all of them. In his 1987 edition of *Models of the Church*, Dulles added a sixth model: the Church as community of disciples. This book established his reputation among Catholics and other Christians in the United States and beyond; it became a widely used textbook for courses in ecclesiology.

Dulles's gift for precise ecclesial thought was again on display in his *Resilient Church* (1977). Envisaging a renewal that did not, however, entail loss of identity, he carefully examined nine crucial issues that have commanded attention since the close of Vatican II: for example, what precisely is the mission of the Church today? What is the role of the pope and Church leadership? How have concepts of Church membership changed? With clarity and boldness, Dulles examined these and further contemporary questions.

Four years younger than Dulles and a fellow American Jesuit, Francis Sullivan, like Dulles, did his doctorate in theology at the Gregorian University. His thesis, *The Christology of Theodore of Mopsuestia* (1956), might have led him to teaching patristics. Instead, he became a professor of ecclesiology at the Gregorian (1956–92), witnessed directly the events of Vatican II, and became, in one famous context, an unofficial adviser to American bishops attending the Council. At a presentation made at the North American College, he recommended that they support a fully New Testament view of personal charisms or special gifts equipping all the baptized to serve in the Church. This teaching was eventually endorsed by *Lumen Gentium* (art. 12), an article partly shaped by a text from Sullivan that an American bishop submitted to the relevant conciliar commission. This meant rejecting Cardinal Ernesto Ruffini's view that charisms were more or less limited to saints and mystics.[15] Sullivan went on to write a classic study in support of the Charismatic Renewal, *Charisms and Charismatic Renewal: A Biblical and Theological Study* (1982).

Around the world, Sullivan's *Magisterium* (1983) became a standard volume about teaching authority in the Catholic Church. He built on this classic study further, after he retired from the Gregorian and taught graduate students at Boston College (1992–2009). *Creative Fidelity: Weighing and Interpreting Documents of the Magisterium* (1996) and *From Apostles to Bishops: The Development of the Episcopacy in the Early Church* (2001) illustrate Sullivan's gift for research and exact thought. *Creative Fidelity* shows how the full authority of the "ordinary," universal magisterium is not invested, for instance, in rejecting either birth control or the admittance of women to the ordained ministry. His article in *Theological Studies* in 1993, "The Secondary Object of Infallibility," had already argued that the sinfulness of contraception has not been infallibly taught and so is reformable.[16]

Some Church leaders and theologians have insisted that the ordinary, universal magisterium of the bishops in union with the Bishop of Rome has *definitively* (but not infallibly) taught that the revelation mediated through Christ excludes the priestly ordination of women. But how do they know this? Canon 749 of the 1983 Code of Canon Law states that "no doctrine is understood to be infallibly [or definitively?] defined unless it is clearly established as such." As Sullivan pointed out, it is not a clearly established fact that the bishops around the world have been *unanimous* and *constant* in teaching that women should be excluded from priestly ordination.[17] Chapter 4 below will take up the objections against the category of "definitive but not infallible" that have been made by the distinguished canon lawyer Ladislas Orsy, SJ. This Hungarian Jesuit taught at the Gregorian University (during Vatican II), Fordham University, Catholic University of America, and Georgetown University.

Another disputed question that Sullivan addressed several times was the interpretation of the verb *subsistit* in Vatican II's Dogmatic Constitution on the Church (*Lumen Gentium* 8). When *Lumen Gentium* stated that "the one Church of Christ subsists in the Catholic Church," the context indicated that this was meant: "the one Church of Christ continues to exist *fully* in the Catholic Church." But the Congregation for the Doctrine of the Faith wanted this statement to mean that "the Church of Christ continues to exist *only* in the Catholic Church." Yet "existing fully" is not the equivalent of "existing only." Several times in *Theological Studies* and elsewhere,[18] Sullivan convincingly ruled out the CDF's repeated, and sometimes inconsistent, attempts to narrow the meaning of *subsistit in*.[19]

Unlike Dulles with his *Models of the Church*, Sullivan never wrote a fundamental ecclesiology as such. He came close, however, with a study of the four essential "marks" or essential qualities of the Church: unity, holiness, catholicity, and apostolicity (*The Church We Believe In: One, Holy, Catholic, and Apostolic*, 1988).

He also explored the relationship to the Church of those who never come to Christian faith and baptism (*Salvation outside the Church? Tracing the History of the Catholic Response*, 1992). This study had an impact on Jacques Dupuis (*Toward a Christian Theology of Religious Pluralism*, 1997) and through him on modern debates in the theology of religions. In a contribution to a Festschrift honoring Dupuis on his eightieth birthday (*In Many and Diverse Ways*, 2003), Sullivan returned to his first love, patristics, contributing a chapter on "Clement of Alexandria and Justification through Philosophy." He investigated how Clement remains pertinent to modern discussions about the salvific function of non-Christian religions.

SACRAMENTAL THEOLOGY AND GRACE

Our next chapter will mention, in the context of pastoral theology, a work of sacramental theology by Theodore Macken (1922–94). Here we should not neglect the teaching and publications of Edward J. Kilmartin (1923–94), John D. Laurance (b. 1938), and other American Jesuits. Kilmartin's most influential book was probably his posthumous *Eucharist in the West: History and Theology* (1998), edited by Robert J. Daly (b. 1933). Laurance taught and wrote on the Eucharist and priesthood. Here we should include Bernard Cooke (1922–2013), who did his doctorate at the Institut Catholique de Paris, taught at Marquette University, left the Society of Jesus in 1969, taught at the Jesuit Holy Cross College, Worcester (MA), and published extensively. His magisterial work in sacramental theology and ecclesiology, *Ministry in Word and Sacraments* (1976), has remained a classic work in that field.

On the theme of grace, the Belgian Piet Fransen, SJ (1913–83), made notable contributions with *Grace and the Sacraments* (1958), *Divine Grace and Man* (1962), and *The New Life of Grace* (1969). As a visiting professor, he was invited to teach at Fordham University, the University of San Francisco, and Loyola University at Chicago.[20]

The influence of Jesuits in sacramental theology and the theology of grace should not be separated from what they achieved in liturgical teaching and studies. This theme will be handled in the next chapter.

PATRISTICS

A 1989 instruction on the study of the Church fathers (issued by the Vatican's Congregation for Education) distinguished *patrology*, the historical and literary study of the Church fathers, from *patristics*, the study of their theological thought. We can happily endorse the distinction, provided we emphasize scholarly *study*. It is one thing to consult a collection of extracts like that provided by Marie Joseph Rouët de Journel, but quite another to undertake the serious work that produced *Sources Chrétiennes*, initiated by Jean Daniélou and other French Jesuits (see chap. 1 above), preparing the way for the teaching of Vatican II.

Chapter 1 of the Decree on the Church's Missionary Activity, *Ad Gentes* (To the Nations), demonstrated how effectively the thought of the fathers can enrich teaching on the Church's mission. Yves Congar, OP, drafted that chapter, the longest of the six chapters that make up *Ad Gentes*. It cited or referred to more sources than all the other chapters taken together. Congar's patristic scholarship was particularly well deployed. In a tour de force, he introduced quotations from or references to twenty-three fathers of the Church, some of them, like Irenaeus and Augustine, more than once. He retrieved remarkable texts that illuminate principles that guide the Church's missionary activity, itself based on the "missionary activity" of the Trinity for the salvation of human beings.[21]

We remarked above on Walter Burghardt's work in patristics (chap. 1); inevitably it came up short. His twenty-three years as editor of *Theological Studies* and, even more, his lifelong commitment to the theory and practice of fruitful preaching limited fuller engagement with the fathers of the Church. Of the more than twenty-five books he wrote and published, fifteen were collections of homilies and sermons. A university survey put him among the twelve most effective preachers in the United States.[22]

Burghardt inspired younger Jesuits to dedicate themselves to patristic scholarship: in particular, Robert J. O'Connell (1925–99), Roland J. Teske (1934–2015), Brian E. Daley (b. 1940), Joseph T. Lienhard (b. 1940), Philip R. Amidon (1943–2020), and J. William Harmless (1953–2014). These American Jesuits also found inspiration in the Jesuit patristic experts in France: (Cardinal) Jean Daniélou (1905–74), (Cardinal) Henri de Lubac (1896–1991), and Henri Crouzel (1918–2003). De Lubac joined Daniélou in founding *Sources Chrétiennes* and went on to publish a landmark work on medieval exegesis, *Exégèse mediévale* (four volumes, 1959–64). His *Corpus Mysticum* (1944) showed how this term had originally (prior to the eleventh century) characterized the Eucharist and not the Church (as in the 1943 encyclical of Pius XII, *Mystici Corporis Christi*). The 2003 encyclical of John Paul II, *Ecclesia de Eucharistia* (the Church from the Eucharist), endorsed the social and ecclesial meaning of the Eucharist as building the Church, a notion that de Lubac had also retrieved. Crouzel, along with other remarkable studies such as an essay on what the early Church held about divorce and remarriage, is remembered for rehabilitating Origen as a genuinely orthodox writer of the third century.

Roland Teske (1934–2015), a professor of medieval philosophy and theology at Marquette University, Milwaukee, specialized not only in William of Auvergne, a bishop of Paris (d. 1249), and Henry of Ghent (d. 1293) but also in Augustine (354–430). By himself or in collaboration, Teske produced significant studies on Augustine's anti-Manichean and anti-Pelagian works. He proved a major figure in the New City Press project of translating into English, with introductions and notes, the surviving writings of Augustine. As well as translating several other works by Augustine, Teske prepared in four volumes a translation of letters, mainly from Augustine but some addressed to Augustine. Teske's contribution has been ranked highly, especially by those who nominate Augustine, Anselm of Canterbury, and Aquinas as the "A" team in Western theology.

Another Jesuit giant in Augustine studies was Robert J. O'Connell of Fordham University, who produced at least seven outstanding books on Augustine: *St. Augustine's Early Theory of Man* (1968); *St. Augustine's Conversion: The Odyssey of Soul* (1969); *Art and Christian Intelligence in Saint Augustine* (1978); *Imagination and Metaphysics in St. Augustine* (1986); *The Origin of the Soul in St. Augustine's Later Works* (1987); *Soundings in St. Augustine's Imagination* (1993); and *Images of Conversion in St. Augustine's Confessions* (1996). Current work on Augustine by a Jesuit of the next generation, David V. Meconi (b. 1965), has been rapidly approaching Teske's and O'Connell's level of achievement.

After teaching at Marquette (1975–90), Joseph Lienhard moved to Fordham University and has remained there, apart from stints as a visiting professor at Boston College and the Gregorian University, Rome. A specialist in the work of Origen and Augustine, he has also expounded the history of patristic exegesis. Doctoral studies at the Universities of Mainz and Freiburg, at a time when German theological scholarship still led the world, enriched Lienhard's formation. His translation of Origen's homilies and fragments on Luke (1996) made him one of the Jesuits involved in producing the prestigious series The Fathers of the Church (Catholic University of America Press, 1947–), which by 2018 numbered 136 volumes.[23] Catholic University of America Press published a Festschrift in honor of Lienhard on the occasion of his seventieth birthday, *Tradition and the Rule of Faith in the Early Church* (2010). He attended two of the four New York "summits" (run by Davis, Kendall, and O'Collins), those on the Trinity and the incarnation, and contributed to *The Trinity* (1999) a learned and insightful chapter on the phrase one *ousia* and three *hypostases* (one being and three subjects or persons), which traditionally has summed up "the Cappadocian settlement" of Trinitarian controversy in the fourth century.

The first Fordham University student to win a Rhodes Scholarship, which took him to the University of Oxford, Brian Daley was to return there (as a Jesuit) to write his DPhil (awarded 1978) under the direction of Henry Chadwick, a world figure in patristic studies and a specialist in Augustine scholarship who valued the work and friendship of Teske. Daley wrote his thesis on Leontius of Byzantium (active fifth to sixth century) and eventually published for Oxford University Press a magisterial edition, with translation and introduction, of the complete works of Leontius (2017).

Prior to his doctoral studies in Oxford, Daley had studied at the Hochschule Sankt Georgen, Frankfurt-am-Main, where he was befriended by Aloys (later Cardinal) Grillmeier (1910–98), a prolific writer who is best known for his monumental study of the development of Christology, *Christ in the Christian Tradition* (vol. 1, 1965, and vol. 2 published in four parts, 1986–96).[24] A *peritus* at the Second Vatican Council, Grillmeier had a hand in drafting four of the Council's sixteen documents. A dedicated ecumenist, he contributed his vast knowledge of ancient teaching and controversies to the mission of the Pro Oriente Institute (Vienna) and its dialogues with the Oriental Orthodox Churches, the Eastern Churches that rejected the Council of Chalcedon (451). This work bore fruit in the official, joint confessions of faith in Christ between the Catholic Church and the Coptic Pope Shenouda III of Egypt (1973), the Assyrian Church of the East (1994), and the Armenian Katholikos Karekin I (1996).

Daley wrote essays in German on patristic soteriology (the work of Christ as Savior)[25] and eschatology (the doctrine of the last things). He followed Grillmeier by building on a deep patristic scholarship to commit himself to dialogue with Eastern Christians. St. Vladimir's Seminary Press published his *On the Dormition of Mary* (1998), a translation of homilies on the Blessed Virgin by Greek Fathers. From 1978 to 1996, Daley taught for the Weston School of Theology, Cambridge, Massachusetts; in 1996 he moved to the theology department at the University of Notre Dame, Indiana. Shortly before his seventieth birthday, the University of Notre Dame Press recognized Daley's contribution to patristic studies and ecumenism by publishing in his honor *In the Shadow of the Incarnation: Essays on Jesus Christ in the Early Church* (2008).

Like Daley, Philip Amidon received a DPhil at Oxford. He has taught at Creighton University, Omaha, and, among other things, done fine work as a translator. For the Fathers of the Church series, he translated in two volumes the *Festal Letters* of Cyril of Alexandria (nos. 118 and 127) and the *Rufinus of Aquileia: History of the Church* (no. 133). William Harmless, another Jesuit to teach at Creighton, specialized in the literature of early monasticism. He presented the desert fathers and published key texts from their writings.

CHURCH HISTORY

The study of Church history maintains its special place in programs of theology. There can be no substitute for an extended tour of the history of Catholicism if we wish to grasp the nature and identity of

Catholicism. Great historians of Christianity, like outstanding Bible scholars, challenge a drift to shallow mediocrity that reduces the value of theological departments and their teaching. Historical scholarship served the worldwide Church by enabling the Second Vatican Council to retrieve valuable but forgotten traditions, for example, the permanent diaconate for married men (*Lumen Gentium* 29) and the Rite of Christian Initiation of Adults (RCIA; *Sacrosanctum Concilium* 64). This scholarship also enabled the bishops at Vatican II to reform teaching on such matters as the Catholic Church's view of Islam and relationship to Muslims (*Lumen Gentium* 16; *Nostra Aetate* 3), as well as on the Catholic relationship with the Jewish people (*Lumen Gentium* 16; *Nostra Aetate* 4). But, in the United States and elsewhere, Church historians themselves had needed challenges.

John Tracy Ellis (1905–92) was a diocesan priest who spent much of his academic life teaching at the Catholic University of America, apart from some years at the (Jesuit) University of San Francisco (1963–76). Editor of the *Catholic Historical Review* from 1941 to 1962, he published in *Thought* (see our preface above) a famous 1952 call to American Catholic historians and other scholars ("American Catholics and the Intellectual Life"). They should measure up to the intellectual standards of their European counterparts. They had been failing to do so.

Directly or indirectly, Ellis encouraged Jesuit superiors in the United States to invest manpower and money in the study of Church history. New generations of Jesuit historians have produced distinguished researchers: for instance, Gerald P. Fogarty (b. 1939; on the American bishops and other themes in U.S. Church history); Charles R. Gallagher (b. 1965; on Vatican diplomacy); Mark S. Massa (b. 1950; on American Catholic history); John W. Padberg (b. 1926; on the founding and current history of Jesuits); Jared Wicks (b. 1929; on the Reformation and Vatican II); Thomas Worcester (b. 1955; on religion and culture in early modern France and Italy); and Oliver P. Rafferty (b. 1956; an Irish-born Jesuit who teaches at Boston College and has written not only on Irish history but also on nineteenth- and twentieth-century Church history). From 1986 to 2014, Padberg directed at Saint Louis University the Institute of Jesuit Sources, which had been founded in 1961. This valuable institute moved in 2014 to Boston College and was renamed the Institute of Advanced Jesuit Studies.

John W. O'Malley (b. 1927), possessing, like Padberg, a PhD in history from Harvard University, has emerged as a towering figure among Jesuit historians. He has produced significant publications on the Renaissance, the Reformation, and the history of the Society of Jesus: for instance, *The First Jesuits* (1993; translated into twelve languages). His work on the past has constantly illuminated the present, and not least his accounts of the sixteenth-century Council of Trent, the First Vatican Council (1869–70), and the Second Vatican Council (1962–65).

His writings on Vatican II have enjoyed a mass appeal: for instance, *What Happened at Vatican II* (2008) has been translated into at least six languages. His knowledge of the Renaissance and early modern sources has yielded insights into the dialogic form of Vatican II's documents.[26] He has sparked further valuable discussions. For instance, his article "Vatican II: Did Anything Happen?" was followed quickly by two scholarly responses: the first, by Stephen Schloesser, SJ, more historical and the second, by Neil J. Ormerod, processing with a Lonergan-style ecclesiology the material offered by O'Malley and Schloesser.[27]

Shortly before O'Malley's seventy-fifth birthday, the University of Toronto Press published a Festschrift in his honor: *Early Modern Catholicism* (2001). In chapter 7, we will fill out what he and other Jesuits in the United States did toward encouraging the interpretation and implementation of the teaching of Vatican II.

When we check the careers of outstanding American Jesuits presented in this chapter, we cannot miss the excellence and variety of the institutions where they studied: Harvard University (Dulles, O'Malley, and Padberg); Fordham University, Oxford University, and Sankt Georgen, Frankfurt (Daley); Stanford (Schloesser); the Gregorian University (Sullivan and Weigel); and top German universities (Lienhard and Wicks). We should not ignore the studies that prepared the modern Jesuit astronomers we cited above: Guy Consolmagno, George Coyne (twenty-eight years as director of the Vatican Observatory), and William Stoeger. Consolmagno studied at the Massachusetts Institute of Technology and the University of Arizona. Coyne studied at Fordham and Georgetown. Stoeger took his PhD at the University of Cambridge, where he was a student of Martin Rees (the Astronomer Royal) and a colleague of Stephen Hawking.

We move next to the record of Jesuits in developing moral theology, liturgy, pastoral theology, and canon law in the United States and elsewhere.

Appendix

"The Martins and the Coys," a popular song about a feud between two mountain families, was recorded by Gene Autry for the 1946 film *Make Mine Music*. It provided the tune for "The Trinity Song," written by Claude R. Daly, SJ (1916–2009), a native of Austin, Texas, who spent many years of priestly ministry in Sri Lanka before returning to the United States in 2003. His verses may wittily sum up early Church doctrine, but they hint at a verbal "orthodoxy" that offers little toward the life of Christian faith. They reflect the standard kind of theology still being taught in those days in many Jesuit theologates.

> Gather round me, children, and I'll teach you doctrine which you must believe if you would save your soul. It's the first and most far-reaching of the truths in Catholic teaching. It's the basis of each part and of the whole.
>
> God the Father, God the Son, God the Spirit—Three are One. Each and all, one God, one Jahweh Elohim, each one has his own subsistence in the one supreme existence. Such a truth no finite mind would ever dream.
>
> Now this mystery is plainly taught in Scripture. Here's the text that all the Fathers cited most: "First, you have to catechize 'em, then with water you baptize 'em, in the name of Father, Son, and Holy Ghost."
>
> God the Father, God the Son, God the Spirit—Three are One: One in nature, one in power, one in name. The baptized are consecrated, marked as sons, regenerated, by three Persons who in essence are the same.
>
> All the early Christians firmly held this dogma, but expounders sometimes went a bit astray. For they all had fussy notions till the three great Cappadocians set them straight and fixed the terms we use today. [St. Basil the Great, his brother St. Gregory of Nyssa, and his friend St. Gregory of Nazianzus are these Cappadocians.]
>
> God the Father, God the Son, God the Spirit—Three are One, as the Church has always publicly professed. Though they slipped when they explained it, all her loyal sons maintained it as her rites and creeds and martyrs all attest.

Bishop Arius said the Son was just a creature. Athanasius worked to lay the scoundrel low, till the Council of Nicea said there's only one "ousia"—you can read the text in DB 54. [Clemens Bannwart edited for a time the collection of church teaching first created by Heinrich Denzinger in 1854; hence DB or Denzinger Bannwart.]

God the Father, God the Son, God the Spirit—Three are One; and the Arian error now is dead and gone. Though they raised an awful cry-out, Athanasius put their "I" out, and proclaimed the Son was *homo-ousion* [= of the same being (with the Father); the Arians weakened the force of the adjective by adding an "I" and speaking of the Son as *homoi-ousion*, of a similar being to the Father].

Eastern Greeks were always fighting with the Romans, finding something wrong with every Latin deed. So some bishopolitician had a pretext for sedition when they added "Filioque" to the Creed. [The Latin Church unilaterally added to the Creed "and from the Son," indicating that the Holy Spirit proceeds from the Father and the Son. Patriarch Photius of Constantinople (d. 895) objected.]

God the Father, God the Son, God the Spirit—Three are One, and the Spirit joins the Father and the Son. He's their equal—they're not higher. But they send Him—they're both prior. He proceeds from each; as principle they're one.

CHAPTER 4

MORAL THEOLOGY, LITURGY, PASTORAL THEOLOGY, AND CANON LAW

THE SECOND VATICAN COUNCIL (1962–65) expected moral theology to be improved by "drawing more fully on the teaching of holy Scripture" (*Optatam Totius* 16). As for the liturgy or the public worship of the Church, two articles of the first document promulgated by the Council (*Sacrosanctum Concilium* 15–16) prescribed improvements in teaching liturgy for seminaries, religious houses of studies, and faculties of theology. In its Decree on the Training of Priests, *Optatam Totius*, Vatican II attended to catechesis, or the instruction preparing candidates for baptism, and deepening faith in those already baptized. The Council also reintroduced the ancient tradition of initiating catechumens or RCIA (*Sacrosanctum Concilium* 64–66), recognized the great value of the ministry of catechists, and emphasized the need to prepare and update them for their ministry (*Ad Gentes* 15, 17). Catechetics remains a major theme for pastoral or practical theology, to which *Optatam Totius* devoted three articles (19–21). *Optatam Totius* (art. 16) also prescribed that courses in canon law were to be enhanced by relating canon law to the "mystery" of the Church as set out in the Council's dogmatic constitution *Lumen Gentium*.

Both before and after Vatican II, what did Jesuits in the United States contribute in these four areas? From the nineteenth century to the opening decades of the twenty-first century, how have they influenced the development of moral theology, liturgy, pastoral theology (including catechesis), and canon law?

MORAL THEOLOGY

As the field of theology that systematically studies and teaches how Christians (and others) ought to live, moral theology draws on the Bible (e.g., the Decalogue, the Sermon on the Mount, and the *parenēsis* of Paul), philosophical ethics, the traditional teaching of the Church, the human sciences, and human experience. It should be based on a full vision of the fashioning and refashioning of humanity. What has creation involved? What has been brought about through the life, death, and resurrection of Christ, the coming of the Holy Spirit, and the birth of the Church?[1]

After St. Thomas Aquinas, moral theology often became isolated from its scriptural and doctrinal roots and at times lapsed into empty legalism. The moral teaching of St. Alphonsus Liguori (1696–1787), marked by great learning and deep pastoral concern, helped initiate change. From the end of the nineteenth century, Jesuit and other moral theologians became challenged and enriched by developments in biblical studies, the human sciences (including history, psychology, and sociology), philosophical pluralism, and perhaps most of all, a doctrinal renewal—in Christology, ecclesiology, and theological anthropology. Since Leo XIII (pope 1878–1903), papal teaching has more and more encouraged moral theologians not only to study questions of individual morality but also to take up wider questions of social justice, church-state relations, international relations, and peace. Vatican II's Constitution on the Church in the Modern World, *Gaudium et Spes* (1965), was the first far-reaching and fairly complete official document on the moral life of Christians and, for that matter, of all human beings. We say, "fairly complete," since *Gaudium et Spes* had nothing to say directly, for instance, about ecological issues.

From the nineteenth century, some American Jesuits were involved in reflection and action that concerned the rights of the migrant working classes. On this and other issues, often without putting matters explicitly and without being professional teachers of moral theology, they tackled this issue: how was papal social teaching to be applied in the American scene? After a very well-attended conference held at West Baden over the Labor Day weekend in 1943, Daniel Lord (1888–1955), supported by John LaFarge (1880–1963), launched the Institute of Social Order (ISO) as a national organization.[2] Back in 1930, Lord had been asked to write a production code for the motion picture industry. But with the ISO and its journal, *Social Order* (published until 1963), his agenda became much broader. He and LaFarge supported the desegregation of Saint Louis University in 1944, which, "without support from peer institutions in the area, took place a decade before the Supreme Court's decision prohibiting segregation in public schools and about fifteen years before the integration of Southern universities got underway."[3]

It was John Courtney Murray (1904–67), editor of *Theological Studies* (1941–67), who left the most enduring monument in the field of social morality promoted by American Jesuits. Research and writing on religious freedom, interracial justice, and church-state relations prepared the way for his work as a *peritus* at Vatican II. Along with Yves (later Cardinal) Congar, Johannes Feiner, and Pietro (later Cardinal) Pavan, he helped draft the Declaration on Religious Liberty, *Dignitatis Humanae*, a document that accepted religious pluralism and a genuine separation of church and state.[4] Congar came to respect and even warmly admire Murray for his noble character and contribution to the Council.[5] Pavan had helped to draft the encyclical of John XXIII, *Pacem in Terris*, which opened the way for Vatican II's Constitution on the Church in the Modern World, *Gaudium et Spes*.

Murray expounded his ideas on religious liberty in *The Problem of Religious Freedom* (1965) and in a book he edited, *Religious Liberty: An End and a Beginning* (1966). A fellow Jesuit recalled how Murray "entered a room like an ocean liner."[6] Far from being lost in a crowd, Murray became the first Jesuit featured on the cover of *Time* magazine (December 12, 1960), the only one before Daniel Berrigan (January 25, 1971), Fr. Pedro Arrupe (April 23, 1973), and Cardinal Jorge Bergoglio, SJ, who became Pope Francis in March 2013 and was selected by *Time* as the man of the year.

American Jesuits took pride in the achievements of John Courtney Murray. At its commencement in May 1966, Gonzaga University conferred an honorary doctorate on him: "There is a distinctive appropriateness in the fact that America, scene of the first great modern experiment in civil liberty, should have been the birthplace of the country's great theologian of religious liberty." The citation compared Murray with (now Saint) John Henry Newman: "The Church's new, dynamic and progressive understanding of man [*sic*!] grows out of notion of the development of doctrine. Like Newman...John Murray had his clouded years, but unlike the English Cardinal he has lived to see his views on Church and State fully exonerated." The citation concluded, "Gonzaga salutes a priest-scholar for his awesome labors in this field, so long neglected in the Church, so important in contemporary American life, so basic for an understanding of Christ's incarnation. In gratitude and appreciation we today declare John Courtney Murray, Doctor of Laws of Gonzaga University and make him our son."

For decades, right up to Vatican II, Jesuits in the United States and other countries studied their moral theology out of manuals, often written in Latin and characterized by abstract principles, an adept use of casuistry,[7] appeals to esteemed moral authors, and some exaggerated claims about allegedly definitive papal teaching. One commonly used (Latin) manual was the two-volume work by Eduard Genicot (1856–1900), Joseph Salsmans (1873–1944), and Albert Gortebecke, *Institutiones Theologiae Moralis*, which had reached its seventeenth edition by 1951.[8] The American Jesuit John Ford (1902–89) belonged to this tradition, but with differences.[9]

With Gerald Kelly, SJ, Ford coauthored a widely used, two-volume work, *Contemporary Moral Theology: Questions in Fundamental Moral Theology*, and *Marriage Questions*. From 1941 to 1954 they also prepared for *Theological Studies* (founded in 1940) the "Notes on Moral Theology," now renamed "Notes on Theological Ethics." During the Second World War (1939–45), Ford was the only American moral theologian to reject obliteration bombing, which systematically destroyed enemy cities. His article in *Theological Studies* (September 1944), "The Morality of Obliteration Bombing," denounced this strategy as violating the right of German citizens to noncombatant immunity.[10] Subsequently he also objected to the use of weapons of mass destruction such as atomic bombs. Ford had the satisfaction of seeing his teaching endorsed by Vatican II: "Every act of war directed to the indiscriminate destruction of whole cities or vast areas with their inhabitants is a crime against God and humanity, which merits firm and unequivocal condemnation" (*Gaudium et Spes* 80).

When John XXIII formed the Papal Commission on Population, Family, and Birth Rate to advise him about teaching on birth control,

Ford was appointed a member. The majority eventually proposed repealing the rejection of contraception. Ford belonged to the minority who argued for no reform. His fellow Jesuit, Josef Fuchs (1912–2005), wrote the majority report. Ford, however, wrote a minority report arguing that change in the teaching would diminish the authority of the magisterium to pronounce on such matters. Such a change would mean admitting error on the part of the Catholic Church and accepting the Protestant position on contraception. Ford contributed to Paul VI's fateful decision to maintain the current teaching and publish in 1968 the encyclical rejecting contraception, *Humanae Vitae* (Of Human Life). Ford supported Cardinal Patrick O'Boyle of Washington (1896–1987), who sanctioned priests in his archdiocese for dissenting from *Humanae Vitae*. Those priests included O'Boyle's own confessor, a Jesuit. In 1978, Ford coauthored with Germain Grisez a lengthy article, "Contraception and the Infallibility of the Ordinary Magisterium,"[11] which claimed that the rejection of contraception had been infallibly taught by the ordinary magisterium of the Catholic Church—a position firmly rejected by Francis Sullivan, SJ, among others (see chap. 3 above).

For the post-Ford generation, Richard A. McCormick, SJ (1922–2000), was a dominant voice by being editor of "Notes on Moral Theology" for *Theological Studies* (1965–84) and coediting eleven volumes on Catholic moral theology. His "Notes" surveyed and evaluated the work of ethicists around the world. He insisted on gathering and assessing evidence, especially in medical ethics. He contributed to the development of thinking about proportionate reason and conscientious dissent. While he completed his 1957 thesis at the Gregorian University with another director, he valued the classes of Josef Fuchs and remained in contact with him.[12]

From his base at Boston College, James F. Keenan, SJ (b. 1953), who also studied with Fuchs in Rome, has continued and extended the work of McCormick. He has written prolifically on virtue ethics, moral methodology, HIV/AIDS, and the modern history of moral theology. Virtue ethics, an approach to ethics derived from Aristotle (384–322 BC), promotes habits that form character and bring about human "flourishing" (in moral communities that shape life for virtuous individuals), rather than highlighting (a) obligations to be fulfilled (deontological ethics), (b) the "useful" consequences of one's actions (utilitarian ethics), or (c) the "loving" context of one's actions (situation ethics).

Some fear that virtue ethics seem to base moral obligations on the likelihood of one's actions bringing true happiness and so reduce moral commandments to being conditional rather than categorical. But Thomas Aquinas emphasizes that virtues are more a gift of God than a human achievement. Supporters of virtue ethics can cite St. Paul's exhortations to practice the virtues of the new life (e.g., Col 3:12–17). The apostle shapes the central questions for virtue ethics: Who *are* we as baptized persons professing hope in the resurrection? What does the risen Jesus want us to *become*?

Keenan has set himself to develop a global and culturally sensitive perspective in moral theology. He founded Catholic Theological Ethics in the World Church, an international network of Catholic ethicists, who have fostered multicultural dialogue on moral issues through meetings in Padua (2006), Trent (2010), and Sarajevo (2018).[13] The association has also sponsored regional meetings. Since 2003, Keenan has been writing the "Notes on Theological Ethics" for *Theological Studies*. In *A History of Moral Theology in the Twentieth Century* (2010), Keenan supplies valuable information about and insights into Jesuit ethical teaching, especially since Vatican II. Most recently, he has produced an excellent article on the role of *Theological Studies* in publishing theological ethics since its foundation in 1940.[14]

The strength of programs in theological ethics at Boston College has come from (a) its attention to biblical sources, the thought of Aquinas, and social teaching, and from (b) the quality of faculty members, like Professor Lisa Sowle Cahill and John J. Paris, SJ (b. 1937). David Hollenbach, SJ (b. 1942), after fruitful years at Weston College (1976–91), taught social ethics at Boston College before moving on to Georgetown University.

Summing up the significant areas in which American Jesuits have contributed to moral theology, we should value what they have done for (a) social ethics (e.g., human rights), (b) bioethics (e.g., in the debate over birth control[15]), and (c) biblical ethics. As for (c), the moral theologian William C. Spohn, SJ (1944–2005), broke new ground with his 1984 book *What Are They Saying About Scripture And Ethics?* Two years later, a notable biblical scholar with strong interests in social justice, John R. Donahue, SJ (b. 1933), called Spohn's work "excellent" when publishing his own fine article, "The 'Parable' of the

Sheep and the Goats: A Challenge to Christian Ethics."[16] The work of Spohn and Donahue in biblical ethics was continued by Yiu Sing Lúcás Chan, SJ (1968–2015), in such works as *The Ten Commandments and the Beatitudes: Biblical Studies and Ethics for Real Life* (2012) and *Biblical Ethics in the 21st Century: Developments, Emerging Consensus, and Future Directions* (2013).[17]

LITURGY

From the time of John Carroll, Jesuits in the United States were the grateful heirs of the Baroque style of Church architecture, support for more frequent Holy Communion, and the practice of various Eucharistic devotions, notably those connected with the Sacred Heart of Jesus.[18]

But in the first half of the twentieth century, apart from Gerald Ellard (1894–1963), few American Jesuits specialized in liturgical scholarship. The European situation was different, with Jesuits like the Austrian Josef Andreas Jungmann (1889–1975) being a towering figure in the liturgical movement that prepared Vatican II's teaching on liturgy.[19] His research resulted in a two-volume history of the Mass, originally published in German (1948); it went through five editions in German, not to mention translations into other languages. A *peritus* at the Council, he helped draft its first document, the Constitution on the Sacred Liturgy, *Sacrosanctum Concilium* (1963).

In the post–Vatican II period, Jesuits were up and running in liturgical teaching and practice in the United States: John F. Baldovin (b. 1947); Keith F. Pecklers (b. 1958), who has influenced the American Church through his writing and teaching at the Gregorian University in Rome; Bruce T. Morrill (b. 1959); Edward Yarnold (1926–2007); and Christopher Willcock (b. 1947).

Baldovin was one of the three associate editors of a learned and critical commentary published by Liturgical Press in 2011 on the unfortunate translation that was imposed in 2010 of the Order of Mass and *The Roman Missal*. For this commentary, Baldovin wrote five sections, all dealing with the history of the Latin text and rite.[20] After earning a PhD at Emory University, Morrill taught at Boston College for fifteen years and is now a professor at Vanderbilt University (Nashville, TN). Coeditor of *The Essential Writings of Bernard Cooke* (2016), he is known for such well-received works as *Divine Worship and Human Healing* (2009) and *Encountering Christ in the Eucharist* (2012).

British born and the first Jesuit to receive a doctorate in theology at the University of Oxford, Yarnold regularly taught courses on liturgy at the University of Notre Dame (Indiana). Willcock, an Australian Jesuit and composer, studied in Paris with Joseph Gelineau, an acclaimed and highly influential Jesuit liturgist and composer.[21] Willcock's antiphons, psalm settings, hymns, and Mass parts have been widely used in the United States and throughout the English-speaking world. In 2013 he composed Masses for Holy Cross College (Worcester, MA) and for Fairfield University (Fairfield, CT). He also composed in 2013 a *Missa Brevis* to celebrate the 750th anniversary of the foundation of Merton College, the Oxford college of Brian Daley before he entered the Society of Jesus (see chap. 3 above).

The giant among American Jesuit liturgists has to be Robert Taft (1932–2018), who taught not only at the University of Notre Dame but also, from 1975 to 2011, at the Pontifical Oriental Institute (Rome). To recognize him as the greatest scholar writing for a Western readership on the liturgies of Eastern Christianity, the Ukrainian Greek Catholic Church elevated him in 1998 to the dignity of an archimandrite. This entitled him to use a miter and a crozier. Many experts believe his six-volume *History of the Liturgy of St. John Chrysostom* to be unsurpassable in its field. In 2001, Taft was instrumental in securing a decree from the Vatican that approved, in certain circumstances, intercommunion between the Catholic Church and the Assyrian Church of the East, an ancient, pre-Chalcedonian church. This involved accepting the validity of the Liturgy of Addai and Mari, a eucharistic prayer addressed not to God the Father but to Christ and lacking the institution narrative, which has normally been considered essential.[22] It was the greatest tribute to his scholarship that Taft ever received. As John Allen wrote, "Taft [had] carved out for himself a unique spot in Rome, based not on careerism but utter and supreme competence."[23]

PASTORAL THEOLOGY

Pastoral theology is concerned with (a) the passage to preaching and catechesis from the study of Scripture and systematic theology, (b) the practice of liturgical and sacramental life, (c) help and counseling for people facing special problems (e.g., the uneducated, drug addicts, refugees, the sick, the old, and the dying), (d) those struggling for justice and peace, and (e) the care (*cura personalis*) of people of different ages and in different life situations.

When opening the Second Vatican Council in 1962, Pope John XXIII expressed his desire for the Council to be characterized by a deeply pastoral tone. By and large the proceedings and teachings of Vatican II adopted a substantial "turn to the pastoral." John O'Malley, SJ, a preeminent commentator on the Council, has repeatedly noted the pastoral style in which it presented the Church's missionary relationship to the wider world. In fact, some of the Vatican II documents, such as *Nostra Aetate* (Declaration on the Relationship of the Church to Non-Christian Religions) and *Ad Gentes* (Decree on the Church's Missionary Activity), owe their existence to the Council's pastoral commitment.

As we saw in chapter 3, the American Jesuit Walter Burghardt gave a lifelong commitment to the theory and practice of effective *preaching*. The New York branch of Herder and Herder also played their part for the American church by publishing translations of German-speaking Jesuits, such as Josef Jungmann (e.g., *Announcing the Word of God*, 1967), Karl Rahner (e.g., *The Church and the Sacraments*, 1963), and Otto Semmelroth (*The Preaching of the Word: On the Theology of Proclamation*, 1965).[24]

St. Ignatius of Loyola insisted that teaching Christian doctrine to children should be a priority for the work of Jesuits. Famous catechisms for children and adults were produced by early Jesuits: for example, St. Peter Canisius (1521–97) and St. Robert Bellarmine (1542–1621).[25] Even if they were not directly involved in its composition, American Jesuits helped to propagate the Baltimore Catechism, by teaching generations of young people to memorize the "correct" answers to questions about the identity of God and the rest. This catechetical method lived on in the work of John Anthony Hardon, SJ (1914–2000). His best-selling *The Catholic Catechism* of 1975 contained over 1,700 questions and answers. More recently, Joseph A. Fitzmyer, SJ (1920–2016), successfully used the question-and-answer method in his best-selling *A Christological Catechism: New Testament Answers* (rev. ed., 1991). Many Jesuits, however, have espoused other pedagogical methods, developed by the Confraternity of Christian Doctrine. They have consistently attended and contributed to the Los Angeles Religious Education Congress, held yearly at Anaheim Conference Center, Anaheim, California, and drawing around forty thousand participants—the largest annual gathering of Catholics in the United States.

A pastoral approach has marked innumerable Jesuits who taught courses on the liturgy and the sacraments at universities, colleges, seminaries, and other centers of theological studies. Here let us mention only one name. Theodore Macken, SJ, after taking his doctorate in sacramental theology at the Gregorian University, taught at Santa Clara University (California) for many years. Year after year he offered a highly popular course, "The Theology of Marriage." Eventually he published *What Is Marriage?* (1982), *Divorce and Remarriage* (1984), and *The Marital Sacrament* (1989). Supplying a wealth of biblical and historical witness (down to and beyond Vatican II's teaching on marriage as a "community of life"), Macken constantly revealed in these three substantial books his concern for pastoral practice and, in particular, for the real needs and questions of married Catholics (and other Christians).

American Jesuits were at the forefront in developing and practicing clinical pastoral education (CPE) and in spreading it elsewhere. To take one example among many, Edwin ("Ned") Cassem, SJ (1935–2015), graduated from Harvard Medical School in 1966 and spent his career as a psychiatrist at Massachusetts General Hospital. He pioneered end-of-life care and became an acclaimed authority on issues concerned with death and dying.

Cassem also served at Harvard University Health Services. Here he was joined for twenty years (1969–89) by another Jesuit MD, the psychiatrist James J. Gill (1925–2003). In 1979, Gill founded an influential journal, *Human Development*. It continues to combine medicine, theology, spirituality, and the social sciences in ways that foster human and spiritual development. Gill himself was ahead of his times through his innovative work for priests with sexual problems.

In 1971, New York Jesuits and their lay associates opened the first Nativity School, which provided a quality education for low-income, often inner-city families who could not pay for private education. In 1996, the first Cristo Rey school opened in Chicago with a similar objective.[26] These developments followed a network of schools for the impoverished, *Fe y Alegría* (Faith and Joy), initiated in 1960 (by a Chilean Jesuit who worked in Venezuela) and subsequently spread throughout

Central and South America.[27] Serious theological reflection on the Church and her mission prompted this commitment to educating the poor. This was nothing less than an exercise of pastoral theology, as was the reflection on the ideals and outcomes to be effected through the programs of these schools.

Leading the way in developing pastoral approaches to those suffering from alcoholism, John Ford drew on his own experience as an alcoholic whose recovery led to contacts with the founders of Alcoholics Anonymous (AA). He spent much time introducing AA to Catholic audiences. He looked on alcoholism as a disease to be treated and not a sin to be judged. "His personal commitment to persons affected by alcoholism," Eric Genilo has written, "is evidenced by long-term work as a telephone counsellor for an alcoholism-counselling service, a ministry that he continued to the age of 86."[28]

Since it was founded in 1981 in Bangkok by the superior general of the Jesuits, Pedro Arrupe (1907–91), the Jesuit Refugee Service has been accepted as part of the Society's apostolic commitment and, not least, by American Jesuits.[29] The desire to serve refugees and asylum seekers expresses a pastoral theology that has pondered the practice of Christian faith and its implications for justice.

Jesuits believe deeply in the power of education to transform societies and individual lives, and this has meant making Jesuit higher education accessible to refugees. Charles Currie (1930–2019) headed the Association of Jesuit Colleges and Universities from 1997 to 2011. After retiring from the association, he became executive director of Jesuit Commons, now called Jesuit Worldwide Learning, which provides online education for students in refugee camps. Regis University in Denver accredits the diplomas and certificates that are granted to those who follow teaching broadcast by Creighton University (Omaha), Fordham, Georgetown, and other Jesuit institutions.

Pastoral theology also involves the personal care (*cura personalis*) of people of various ages and in different life situations: for instance, teenagers and young adults. Daniel Lord proved a giant in pastoral theology at the service of the young.[30] Appointed national director of the Sodality of the Blessed Virgin Mary in 1925, he remained in that post until 1948 and saw members of the sodality at Jesuit high schools, colleges, and universities grow to more than two million. He developed the sodality's magazine, *The Queen's Work*, and aimed at placing this tool of catechesis and evangelization in the hands of every Catholic student in the United States. An accomplished pianist and popular writer, Lord promoted prayer, healthy family life, and all manner of moral values. He wrote fifty-eight musicals, with a message of living the faith in the public square.

After serving as a consultant for the 1927 film *The King of Kings*, Lord became an outspoken member of the Legion of Decency and developed a production code for motion pictures to influence them for the good. Even if this initiative faltered, Lord remained unmatched in communicating with pastoral efficacy to an entire generation of young people.

Recently, pastoral reflection and commitment drove Gregory ("Greg") J. Boyle, SJ (b. 1954), into a ministry for young people in Los Angeles who were involved in gang violence. In 1988 he led others in founding what became Homeboy Industries, the largest gang intervention, rehabilitation, and reentry program in the world.

Those struggling for justice and peace have found champions among American Jesuits, not least Daniel Joseph Berrigan (1921–2016). An outstanding author (around fifty published books) and award-winning poet, he spoke, wrote, and acted effectively for the anti–Vietnam War movement. In 1965 at the Church Center for the United Nations (New York), along with Richard John Neuhaus and Rabbi Abraham Joshua Heschel, he founded Clergy and Laymen Concerned About Vietnam (CALCAV). They were joined by Hans Morgenthau, Reinhold Niebuhr, and William Sloane Coffin. Martin Luther King Jr. delivered a 1967 speech called "Beyond Vietnam: A Time to Break Silence" and served as the organization's national cochairman. On May 17, 1968, with one of his brothers and seven other Catholics, Berrigan led the Catonsville Nine, a group that used homemade napalm to destroy 378 draft files taken from the draft board in Catonsville, Maryland. Convicted at the trial that followed, Berrigan spent four months underground as the first priest on the FBI's "most wanted list" before being arrested, jailed in the federal penitentiary in Danbury (Connecticut), and released on February 24, 1972.[31] *The Trial of the Catonsville Nine*, written by Berrigan himself, performed in New York City, and winning a Tony Award for its director, was produced as a film by Gregory Peck in 1972.

In 1980 Berrigan once again drew the spotlight by founding the Plowshares Movement, an antinuclear warfare group. The Plowshares Eight (Berrigan and seven others) on September 9, 1980, entered a nuclear missile facility in King of Prussia (Pennsylvania), poured blood on documents, and damaged the nose cones of nuclear warheads. Ten years of trials, sentencing, and appeals ended with the group paroled in view of time already served in prison. A 1982 film, *King of Prussia* (starring Martin Sheen), re-created dramatically the legal battle.

By teaching at Union Theological Seminary, Columbia, Cornell, Yale, and—for many years—Fordham, Berrigan spread his message of social and political justice. He also enjoyed the support of friends across the world. Jeremy Irons helped make him a consultant for *The Mission*, a 1986 film (starring Irons and Robert De Niro) about the expulsion of the Jesuits in the eighteenth century from their missions in South America. Berrigan appeared in the film and uttered only one word, "No." His consistent life ethic said no to war, abortion, capital punishment, and cultures that solve problems by killing people. Saying yes to life, Berrigan spent much of his later years ministering to people in the New York area suffering from HIV/AIDS. His active and articulate pastoral theology on behalf of life reached out to millions within the United States and beyond.

Some readers may be surprised by what we have brought together to show how Jesuits contributed to pastoral theology in the United States. But, if one follows Rahner and endorses a broad version of pastoral theology as being practical theology, difficulties vanish.[32] We can recognize, for instance, the theological ministry of Berrigan as an eminent exercise of pastoral/practical theology.

What Berrigan taught and did against war and for peace, life, and justice found its counterpart in the activity of other Jesuits on behalf of the people of Central America and South America. In November 1989, six Jesuits who taught at the University of Central America (San Salvador) were murdered, along with their housekeeper and her daughter, by American-backed military forces. Charles Currie organized the response of Jesuits across the United States. He then helped coordinate the Ignatian Family Teach-In, a yearly event that brought to Washington two thousand young people (from Jesuit colleges, high schools, and parishes) to receive training in social justice.

Here we should also recall Drew Christiansen (b. 1945). As editor of *America* (2005–12), Distinguished Professor of Ethics and Human Development in Georgetown's School of Foreign Service, lecturer, and writer, he has promoted the cause of peacemaking, nuclear disarmament, nonviolence, and social justice. He served on the Atlantic Council's

Middle East Task Force and on the Holy See's delegation that shared in negotiating the Treaty on the Prohibition of Nuclear Weapons during the summer of 2017.

CANON LAW

Jesuits who were canon and civil lawyers for many decades played their part in educating American seminarians and others, either at home in the United States or abroad.[33] Timothy Lincoln Bouscaren (1884–1971), a state attorney general turned Jesuit, taught canon law at St. Mary of the Lake (Mundelein), the Gregorian University, and the Jesuit theologate of West Baden. A distant relative of President Abraham Lincoln, Bouscaren was the first Jesuit canon lawyer to become eminent in the United States.

The Code of Canon Law: A Text and Commentary (1985), commissioned by the Canon Law Society of America on the occasion of the new Latin code of 1983, had twenty-four contributors, three of them Jesuits: Richard A. Hill (1928–2000), James E. Risk (1903–93), and the Hungarian-born Ladislas Orsy (b. 1921). All three canon lawyers did their doctorates at the Gregorian University, while Orsy and Risk also taught there.

We should not pass over in silence other American Jesuits who taught canon law, worked on various tribunals, and were called in as consultors for ecclesial and civil bodies. Robert J. Kaslyn (1956–2019) was a shining example of such ministry. He received his doctorate from Saint Paul University (Ottawa) and published his dissertation, with a foreword by Avery (later Cardinal) Dulles, *Communion with the Church and the Code of Canon Law*. After teaching canon law at the Weston School of Theology (Cambridge, Massachusetts), he joined the faculty of Catholic University of America in 2001 and served as dean of the School of Canon Law (2009–16). He was a member of canon law societies of America, Australia and New Zealand, Canada, and Great Britain and Ireland. Tributes that followed his sudden and untimely death spoke of him as a serious scholar, treasured teacher, and devoted priest.

We should not forget other American Jesuit canon lawyers like James J. Conn (b. 1948), Robert J. Geisinger (b. 1958), and Michael P. Hilbert (b. 1951). They all taught canon law at the Gregorian

University; Geisinger continues to do so. Conn became a professor at Boston College.

Before presenting some highlights of Orsy's story, let us recall Robert Drinan, SJ (1920–2007).[34] Serving as professor and dean of Boston College School of Law (1955–70), in 1970 Drinan was elected to the House of Representatives as a Democrat from Massachusetts. In a speech before the House on July 31, 1973, he called for impeachment proceedings against President Richard Nixon. Drinan's campaign had focused on the need for morality and transparency in U.S. foreign policy, especially in Southeast Asia. The president had been less than honest about bombing raids on Cambodia.

What brought Drinan more into public controversy was his defense of state laws guaranteeing access to abortion. The 1973 *Roe v. Wade* decision of the U.S. Supreme Court saw him distinguish what is immoral from what is illegal, abortion as a sin (in religious morality) but not as a crime (in the area of civil law in a pluralist society). Here the whole issue of the relationship between religious morality and civil law remains controversial in the United States and beyond.

On the occasion of his joining Benjamin Franklin for a mission to Canada on behalf of the Continental Congress, John Carroll expressed his doubts about clergy ever being directly involved in political affairs.[35] But Drinan lasted ten years in the House of Representatives before withdrawing from the 1980 election. He was one of the priests in several parts of the world whose "cases" prompted canon 285 of the 1983 Code of Canon Law (prohibiting clerics from taking public office), even if, as Thomas Massaro observes, "the regulation has been enforced selectively."[36]

As the first Catholic priest ever elected to Congress, Drinan is remembered more for the controversies in which he was involved during his ten years in office rather than for what he did after 1980 by advocating for nuclear disarmament, peace, religious freedom, and justice for migrants.

Orsy not only received a doctorate in canon law from the Gregorian (1954) but also an MA in civil law from the University of Oxford (1960). He taught at the Gregorian (during the Second Vatican Council), later at the Catholic University of America, at Fordham, and, finally (for many years), at Georgetown Law Center. His longstanding authority as a canon lawyer proved itself in challenges to Cardinal

Joseph Ratzinger and in his argument that a bishop of Phoenix had been mistaken in pronouncing on an alleged excommunication.

In an article that originally appeared in 1997, "Justice in the Church: The Legal Wisdom of our Age,"[37] Orsy demonstrated how the procedures followed by the Congregation for the Doctrine of the Faith were not in accord with proper principles of justice: for instance, the right of those accused to be present, to know their accusers, and to defend themselves (or to be represented by someone of their own choice) right from the time when their case began to be heard. As far as we know, neither the CDF nor Cardinal Ratzinger (its prefect) ever replied to this article by Orsy. Far from being something new in the Catholic Church, the provisions proposed by Orsy had been substantially laid down at the Fourth Lateran Council in 1215 by Pope Innocent III:

> He who is the object of an inquiry should be present at the process, and, unless absent through contumacy, should have the various headings of the inquiry explained to him, so as to allow him the possibility of defending himself; as well, he is to be informed not only of what the various witnesses have accused him but also of the names of those witnesses.

When St. Paul defended himself before Agrippa (Acts 25:13—26:32), the Roman prefect Porcius Festus told King Agrippa, "The chief priests and the elders of the Jews informed me about him [Paul] and asked for a sentence against him. I told them that it was not the custom of the Romans to hand over anyone before the accused had met the accusers face to face and been given an opportunity to make a defense against the charge" (Acts 25:15–16). Roman law offered an early precedent or at least intimation for what Orsy argued.

In 1998, Pope John Paul II issued a *motu proprio* (personal decree) in the form of an apostolic letter, *Ad Tuendam Fidem* (For Defending the Faith).[38] The CDF published, in English and several other languages, a commentary (signed by Cardinal Ratzinger) that aimed at explaining more fully the apostolic letter. *Stimmen der Zeit*, a German, Jesuit journal, then featured a debate between Orsy and the cardinal, which is now available in an English translation.[39] Initially, the cardinal peppered his text with criticisms of Orsy: for introducing "a groundless division between two kinds of knowledge," making a "groundless assertion of oppositions," "proceeding somewhat carelessly," and even bringing in "some rather grave errors."

The issue was the addition to canon law of a new category of "definitive teaching," which theologians were obliged to affirm, under pain of sanctions. This new category affirmed the existence of teaching that was irreformable and irreversibly embedded in official teaching and that yet remained distinct from infallible teaching. Questioning "any real difference between infallible" and "definitive" statements," Orsy pointed out that "definitive," "irreformable," and "infallible" are in theory interchangeable. In fact, "a new and vast field for infallible teaching" was being opened up: "the pope is infallible [not only when he teaches *ex cathedra*, as explained by the First Vatican Council, but also] whenever he intends to make a definitive statement." "Official documents of the Holy See" were proposing a new category of irreformable, definitive teaching, which "no pope or council had infallibly approved of." Orsy's argument has never been convincingly answered either by Cardinal Ratzinger or anyone else.

In 2010 the Catholic bishop of Phoenix (Arizona) declared that Sr. Margaret Mary McBride, a religious sister who worked in hospital ministry, had incurred an automatic excommunication for allegedly cooperating in procuring an abortion. A letter from Orsy set the record straight.[40] The declaration by the bishop was itself null and void. Orsy stood tall for his theological and canonical learning, no less than for his outspoken courage.

A CODA

Chapters 3 and 4 have concentrated on *areas* of theology. But there are also movements or *approaches* to theology, such as liberation theology and feminist theology, to which Jesuits in the United States have made their contribution.

Liberation theology has been a largely Latin American movement that (a) is inspired by the exodus, prophetic calls for justice, and Jesus's proclamation of the kingdom; (b) reads the Bible through the lens of integral liberation; and (c) has struck deep roots where structures of injustice and economic dependence oppress great masses of poor people. Its better exponents include Juan Luis Segundo, SJ (1925–96),

Jon Sobrino, SJ (b. 1938), and, above all, Gustavo Gutiérrez, OP (b. 1928), whose *A Theology of Liberation* (original ed. 1972) launched the movement. Deeply concerned with the public function of theology in encouraging social change, the leaders of this movement have developed a spirituality of liberation.

Two years before *A Theology of Liberation* first appeared, *Theological Studies* published Gutiérrez's "Notes for Liberation Theology."[41] From the 1970s, this Jesuit quarterly also presented the views of Segundo, Sobrino, and other liberation theologians.[42] Years later Gutiérrez and Sobrino both featured in a special issue (June 2009) on globalization.

The November 1989 murder of Ignacio Ellacuría, SJ, along with five other Jesuits, their housekeeper, and her daughter, dramatically increased American Jesuit interest in and support for liberation theology. At the Jesuit University of San Francisco, a small garden and plaques recall these victims of American-backed military forces in El Salvador. Jesuit institutions across the United States have kept alive the memory of Ellacuría and his companions—through memorials, courses, and library holdings. Sobrino, who escaped death only because he was away visiting refugee camps, had joined Ellacuría in producing *Mysterium Liberationis*, a two-volume work that presented the fundamental concepts of liberation theology. This and other books by Ellacuría have been translated from Spanish into English and published in the United States. With *The Ground Beneath the Cross: The Theology of Ignacio Ellacuría* (Georgetown University Press, 2000) and subsequent publications, Kevin F. Burke, SJ, has promoted the liberation theology proposed by Ellacuría.[43]

Feminist theology developed largely in the United States since 1968 and has protested against the longstanding masculine bias in Christian theology, exegesis, and church life. It demands the ordination of women, the involvement of women in church governance, and the use of an inclusive language that does not reflect and support a male power structure.

It was not until 1972 that the Jesuit-controlled *Theological Studies* published its first article by a woman theologian, who also happened to be a strong feminist.[44] Three years later Rosemary Radford Ruether was one of the seven women theologians, along with Raymond Brown and George Tavard, who discussed women's ministry, social status, relationships, contemporary consciousness, and similar themes in a special number of *Theological Studies*.[45]

More important, Jesuit universities and colleges began recruiting women theologians (including feminists) for their departments of theology and religious studies. Catherine Cornille and Lisa Sowle Cahill, for example, are among the most distinguished theologians at Boston College.

CHAPTER 5

BIBLICAL STUDIES AND AMERICAN JESUITS

AT THE GENERAL CONGREGATIONS of the Second Vatican Council (1962–65), all held in St. Peter's Basilica, the Book of the Gospels was solemnly enthroned each day, right through the four sessions.[1] Symbolizing the presence of Christ, the book put on display from October 1962 what the Dogmatic Constitution on Divine Revelation, *Dei Verbum* (*DV*) (the Word of God), was to announce three years later about the bishops' teaching office: "[The magisterium] is not above the word of God, but serves it" (*DV* 10). That document began by describing the Council as "Hearing the Word of God with reverence and proclaiming it with faith" (*DV* 1). It ended by stating that "like the Christian religion itself, all the preaching of the church must be nourished and regulated by Sacred Scripture" (*DV* 21). This all-embracing statement also included theology. Vatican II described the task of theology and did so through the image of foundational, strengthening, and rejuvenating functions: "Sacred theology rests upon the written word of God, together with sacred tradition, as its primary and perpetual foundation," and it is "most powerfully strengthened and constantly rejuvenated by that word." Hence, "the study of the sacred page is, as it were, the soul of sacred theology" (*DV* 24).

Vatican II drew this image of Scripture's role as the soul of theology from an 1893 encyclical of Pope Leo XIII (*Providentissimus Deus* 16). In his turn, Leo had taken the image from an early Jesuit source.[2] In the context of this book, we face questions: From the nineteenth century until now, have Jesuits in the United States let the inspired Scriptures serve as the soul of their theology? Did their biblical experts help theologians to do so, as well as prompting the teaching and preaching by bishops and others into becoming more deeply nourished and ruled by the Bible? Did they ever regain the full confidence in the transforming power of the Scriptures that characterized St. Ignatius Loyola and his first companions?

FROM JOHN CARROLL TO THE CATHOLIC BIBLICAL ASSOCIATION

Almost all the early Jesuits lectured on books of the Bible: for instance, St. Francis Borgia, Nicholas Bobadilla, Diego Lainez, and Alfonso Salmeron. Salmeron drew on his own preaching notes and wrote a sixteen-volume commentary on the NT. "Propagating faith by the ministry of the word" was an essential part of the ministry for the first Jesuits (*Formula of the Institute of the Society of Jesus*, approved by Pope Paul III in 1540, 1). When he wrote the *Constitutions*, Ignatius required Jesuit colleges and universities to provide lectures on the OT and NT and have professors of Greek and Hebrew (iv.12, 14). The *Ratio Studiorum* of 1599, which standardized the aim, content, and methods of Jesuit education, mandated that the professors who expounded the Bible should "explain the Sacred Scriptures reverently, learnedly, and seriously according to their genuine and exact sense." They were to avoid the Scholastic method and pursue a literary and theological approach.

Up to the time of the suppression of the Society of Jesus in 1773, there were many Jesuit biblical scholars, most notably the Spaniard Juan Maldonado ("Maldonatus") (1533–83) and the Belgian Cornelius a Lapide (1567–1637). The work of Maldonatus "went far towards rescuing Catholic theology from the barbarous language and barrenness of ideas then prevalent, and his commentaries on the Gospels...are held deservedly in high repute."[3] Cornelius a Lapide produced a ten-volume commentary that covered all the books of the Bible, except Job and the Psalms. His works "have owed their enduring popularity" to "their clarity, deep spirituality," and occasional use of allegorical and other traditional "senses," all "buttressed by a wide erudition" that enabled him to "draw extensively on the Fathers and on medieval theologians."[4] From their foundation to their suppression, Jesuits cherished the ministry of expounding the Bible.

But after the Society of Jesus was fully restored in 1814, scholarly engagement with the Bible came slowly. From the time of John Carroll until the foundation of the Catholic Biblical Association (CBA) of America in 1937, Jesuits in the United States had little to show for themselves in developing and promoting life-giving biblical studies. Many seemed to have little confidence in the transforming power available to those who studied, heard, preached, and prayed over the Bible.[5]

Carroll himself supported the 1790 publication in Philadelphia of the Douay Bible, the first Catholic Bible to be printed in the United States. He wanted to provide a Catholic Bible for his people and shield them against the Protestant King James or Authorized Version.[6]

The Douay Bible is more accurately called the Douay-Reims Bible, since it was produced by scholars of the English College, normally located in Douay but transferred briefly to Reims (1578–93). It was in Reims that they finished and published in 1582 their translation of the NT. Their version of the OT did not appear until 1609–10, years after they had returned to Douay. The translations of both the NT and OT were made from the (Latin) Vulgate rather than from the original languages (Hebrew, Greek, and Aramaic). It was a revised version of the Douay-Rheims Bible that Carroll promoted. It was almost exclusively used in the American Catholic Church until 1941, when at least its translation of the NT was replaced by a revision prepared by the Confraternity of Christian Doctrine.

After its foundation in 1869, Woodstock College did not welcome historical-critical biblical scholarship, even in its better forms. Born in Germany but entering the Society of Jesus in the United States, Anthony J. Maas, SJ (1859–1927), taught Sacred Scripture at Woodstock (1891–1905) and at times engaged in diatribes against biblical criticism. Like many Catholics and other Christians of his time (and later), he was preoccupied with the relationship between the inspiration and the inerrancy of the Bible. The nonbiblical term *inerrancy* betrayed and betrays an apologetical desire to defend the Scriptures against charges of error. The biblical term *truth*, however, expounds matters positively. Being inspired by God, the Bible is true and therefore life-giving.

Maas himself harmonized the four Gospels to publish his *Life of Jesus Christ according to the Gospel History* (1891). In *The Quest of the Historical Jesus* (German original, 1906), Albert Schweitzer brilliantly critiqued major nineteenth-century writers whose so-called lives of Jesus fatally harmonized and modernized the account of Jesus provided by the four Gospels. As well as hitting home against Protestant authors, Schweitzer's criticisms also told against Maas and other Catholics who misguidedly set themselves to write "a" or even "the" life of Christ.

Being a generalist rather than simply a "specialist" on the NT, Maas also published *Christ in Type and Prophecy* (1893), a book aimed at interpreting the OT "factually" or *au pied de la lettre*. In an article that appeared in the same year, Maas insisted, for instance, on taking as historical the story of Eve being fashioned from the rib of Adam (Gen 2:21–22). This was, he argued, true history and not mythical allegory.[7]

In 1900, the editor of the *American Ecclesiastical Review* invited Maas to be the exclusive (and anonymous) writer of the journal's "Recent Bible Study."[8] In the *Messenger of the Sacred Heart* (see chap. 1 above), Maas and some of his Jesuit colleagues had already been sniping at critical biblical scholarship. They "created a caricature of biblical criticism and sought to ensure that several generations of the American Catholic clergy were kept ignorant of the biblical movement."[9] When Maas was appointed superior of the Maryland–New York Province in 1912, one of his disciples, Walter Drum, SJ, took over "Recent Bible Study" and added new targets for his objections, including such moderate English Jesuit commentators on the Bible as Cuthbert Lattey (1877–1954) and C. C. Martindale (1879–1963).[10]

Maas, Drum, and their colleagues reflected, of course, the current limits and weakness of Jesuit biblical studies that extended far beyond the United States. Their attacks on biblical criticism mirrored similar attacks mounted by fellow Jesuits at the Gregorian University in Rome. Prominent among the Roman detractors was Louis Billot, SJ (1846–1931). He wrote his theological manuals in elegant Latin but, when rejecting contemporary scholars, proposed rigid, nonhistorical answers to questions about biblical inspiration and truth. His speculations disdained the evidence of history.[11] The Society of Jesus did not enjoy pioneering scriptural experts like Marie-Joseph Lagrange, OP (1855–1938). He also came under fire from Billot, Maas, and Drum, who felt that Catholic doctrine was threatened by the new historical approach to the Bible. It was not Christian faith but their version of Christian faith that was being challenged by historical criticism.

In 1893 Lagrange founded the École Biblique in Jerusalem. That same year Leo XIII published an encyclical on the study of the Holy Scripture, *Providentissimus Deus*. We have already noted one valuable item in the encyclical that would be taken up by Vatican II, the image of the study of the Bible being the very "soul of theology" (*Dei Verbum* 24; *Optatam Totius* 16). The encyclical also refused to *identify* the divine activity of inspiration with the "inerrancy" of the Scriptures. The Bible is inspired and, therefore, free from error—a teaching that Vatican II adopted but changed by adding the (positive) language of saving truth to the negative language of inerrancy: the books of the Bible "solidly, faithfully and without error [teach] that *truth*, which God wanted put in sacred writings for the sake of our salvation" (*DV* 11). The truth of the Bible results from its being inspired; it is not to be identified tout court with inspiration.

Pope Leo's encyclical did not, however, anticipate what Pius XII in 1943 (*Divino Afflante Spiritu* 33) and Vatican II in 1965 (*DV* 11) did by recognizing that the human authors of the Bible made "use of their powers and abilities." Rather, it used a neo-Scholastic, mechanical scheme of understanding, willing, and acting: "They, first, rightly understood [what God wanted them to think and write], then willed faithfully to write down [these thoughts], and finally expressed [them] in apt words" (*Providentissimus Deus* 20). What many biblical writers (e.g., Luke and the anonymous author of 2 Maccabees) say about their work does not correspond to any such abstract scheme of understanding, willing, and acting.[12] This scheme also reduces drastically the activity of the sacred authors. It comes close to implying that God supplied the ideas to be understood; the human writers then cast around for appropriate words to express these ideas. That part of the encyclical was drafted by Cardinal Camillo Mazzella, who repeated language from the late Cardinal Johann Baptist Franzelin.[13] When Woodstock College opened in 1869, Mazzella, as we saw in chapter 1, had been its first prefect of studies and first professor of dogmatic theology before leaving for Rome at the invitation of Pope Leo XIII. Through a papal encyclical, a former professor of Woodstock influenced worldwide Catholic thinking on the composition of the Bible.

The Vatican-centered campaign against so-called Modernism, authorized by the papal encyclical *Pascendi Dominici Gregis* and the

Holy Office's condemnation of "Modernists," *Lamentabili*, both of 1907, inhibited biblical scholarship everywhere. The previous year the Papal Biblical Commission had declared that Moses was "substantially" the author of the first five books of the Bible. (By that time, most scholars had found this position to be incompatible with the historical evidence; the Pentateuch was composed from several sources and put together after the time of Moses.) But, coupled with the Biblical Commission's "assertion of the Mosaic authorship of the Pentateuch, the encyclical (*Pascendi*) virtually destroyed the Catholic use of the historical method in biblical studies."[14]

Some years earlier, rejection of biblical criticism became intertwined with attacks on so-called Americanism, an ill-defined movement among Catholics who were open to the best insights of the Enlightenment, incipient ecumenism, contemporary culture, and the thought of Fr. Isaac Hecker (1819–88), the founder of the Paulist Fathers.[15] In *Testem Benevolentiae* (January 1899), a document prepared by Cardinal Mazzella, Leo XIII censured a distorted version of "Americanism." Some of the themes of Americanism, such as religious liberty, were vindicated at the Second Vatican Council.

In 1909, Pius X founded the Pontifical Biblical Institute and entrusted it to the Society of Jesus. But for years the Biblicum embraced and taught precritical approaches to the Scriptures.[16] Jesuit professors at the Biblicum and the Gregorian bear some of the blame for the bleak "state of Catholic Biblical scholarship in the United States at the end of the 1930s. Whatever scholarship there had been at the beginning of the century had either been destroyed in the wake of Modernism or had gone underground."[17]

FROM THE LATE THIRTIES UNTIL VATICAN II

After the Jesuit Augustin (later Cardinal) Bea (1881–1968) became rector of the Biblicum in 1930, a renewal of scriptural scholarship in the Catholic Church began again but came slowly.[18] Appointed to the Biblical Commission in 1931 and a friend (later confessor) of Pius XII (pope from 1939), Bea played a significant role in drafting *Divino Afflante Spiritu*.[19] This 1943 encyclical encouraged Catholic scriptural scholars to accept and practice the best of modern biblical criticism. Twenty-five years later, the encyclical's momentous and enduring significance prompted editors Raymond Brown, SS, Joseph Fitzmyer, SJ, and Roland Murphy, OCarm., to gratefully dedicate to the memory of Pius XII their 1968 landmark volume, *Jerome Biblical Commentary*, and to ask Cardinal Bea to write a foreword to the volume. It sold over three hundred thousand copies in the United States and Canada alone.[20]

By 1943, the Catholic Biblical Association of America was still in its formative years.[21] Founded in 1936, with much encouragement from Bishop, later Archbishop, Edwin V. O'Hara (1881–1956)[22] and holding its first general meeting in 1937, the CBA elected William McGarry, SJ (of Weston College), one of its two vice presidents. In 1939 the CBA began publishing the *Catholic Biblical Quarterly*, with a Jesuit, John J. Collins (1900–1991), among those who wrote an article for the second issue. Michael J. Gruenthaner, SJ (1887–1962), became its second editor in 1942. At the outset, the *CBQ* intended to publish popular as well as scholarly articles. In 1950 Edward F. Siegman (1908–67) replaced Gruenthaner and remained editor until 1958. He firmly opted for scholarly articles and reviews. Eventually a popular monthly, *The Bible Today* (published by Liturgical Press, Collegeville, MN), would share biblical developments with a wider public. An influential Canadian Jesuit, David M. Stanley (1914–96), contributed to the first issue of *The Bible Today* (October 1962). Articles quickly came from other Jesuits (of whom more later): for instance, Luis Alonso-Schökel, Frederick Moriarty, and Robert North.

From 1943, the *CBQ* included a "Survey of Periodicals," which led to the creation in 1956 of a separate journal, *New Testament Abstracts*, with Walter M. Abbott, SJ (1923–2008), its founder and first managing editor.[23] Completing his licentiate in theology at Weston College, he handed the *NTA* over to John J. Collins, SJ, who exercised the editorship for a decade. He was followed (1966–1972) by George W. MacRae, SJ (1928–95). Then Daniel Harrington, SJ (1940–2014), took over *NTA* until his death. Collins, MacRae, and Harrington (of whom more later) taught New Testament at Weston College (renamed the Weston Jesuit School of Theology and now Boston College School of Theology and Ministry). Harrington's forty-two-year tenure at *NTA* ensured the journal's indispensability worldwide for New Testament professors and students. The journal is a valuable service to the scholarly community, containing abstracts in English not only of articles written in English but also of articles on New Testament issues written in French, German, Italian, Spanish, and a dozen other foreign languages.

The CBA intended to sponsor summer institutes that could spread a richer knowledge of the Bible among priests, religious, and laypeople. A couple of such institutes took place: in Buffalo (1946) and Denver (1947). But universities, colleges, and seminaries soon engaged themselves in this work, including such Jesuit institutions as Boston College, Fairfield University, Gonzaga University, and the University of San Francisco. Through their summer programs, Jesuits set themselves to create a biblically literate public. They invited fellow Jesuits, like Carlo Maria Martini (Biblicum) and Luis Alonso-Schökel (another professor at the Biblicum), to enrich the programs. Both of us (Kendall and O'Collins) recall with joy how Alonso-Schökel not only taught highly appreciated courses on the Scriptures at the University of San Francisco but also spent time playing a grand piano, filling the Jesuit community house with the sound of music.

Jesuits were also to teach at summer programs organized by others. For twenty-five years (1966–90) at Trinity College in Burlington, Vermont, a Sister of Mercy, Miriam Ward, organized superbly an annual biblical institute. It brought together four or five lecturers to present the best Catholic, Protestant, and Jewish biblical scholarship to an average audience of well over 150 participants. The eventual list of sixty-three faculty members reads like a Who's Who of the contemporary biblical world: from John Bright, Raymond Brown, and Reginald Fuller, through Bruce Metzger, Roland Murphy, Carolyn Osiek, and Pheme Perkins, to Donald Senior and George Ernest Wright. For some years after completing his PhD at the University of Cambridge in 1968, O'Collins taught NT Scripture as well as theology. Thanks to George MacRae, who also lectured for the Trinity College biblical institute,[24] Sr. Miriam invited O'Collins to join her team for several summers.[25]

The above list includes several notable non-Catholic biblical scholars: Bright, Fuller, Metzger, and Wright. They represented the ecumenical context in which many Jesuits and other Catholics now studied and taught the Scriptures. William Foxwell Albright (1891–1971), widely judged in those days to be the leading American specialist on the ancient Middle East, deserves some credit for this development. In 1944 he addressed the annual meeting of the CBA; his paper, "The

Old Testament and Canaanite Language and Literature," subsequently appeared in the *CBQ*, the first article by a non-Catholic published by the journal.

Albright was to help Catholic biblical scholarship in the United States join forces with Protestant experts and gain recognition from them. During the Second World War, he began sharing in the training of a new generation of scriptural scholars, both Jesuits and others. He recalled meeting in the Oriental Institute of Johns Hopkins University (Baltimore) the first Jesuit who came to study with him. In an obituary of Roger T. O'Callaghan, SJ, coauthored with George S. Glanzman, SJ (1916–77), and others, Albright wrote,

> I can never forget a day in early September, 1942, when a tall and handsome young Jesuit came to my office and said he wished to study "the historical background of Scripture." As usual, I gave him an immediate informal quiz, and was delighted to find that he possessed a fluent command of French, German, Italian, and Spanish, as well as the classical languages. Before the end of the year he was speaking Hebrew and Arabic, and had acquired a fair reading knowledge of several other Semitic languages.[26]

Here was a new breed of American Jesuits and others, who earned degrees in ancient Near Eastern languages at Johns Hopkins and then took their doctoral degree elsewhere, often at a secular institution. MacRae, for instance, studied with Albright and then took his doctorate at the University of Cambridge in 1966. Some, like Mitchell Dahood, SJ (1922–82), not only studied at Johns Hopkins but also took his doctorate there. Albright's "work in archaeology and ancient Near Eastern languages provided an irenic milieu in which Catholics could study what had previously been so controversial—the historical background of the Scripture."[27]

Studies at Johns Hopkins prepared Joseph A. Fitzmyer, SJ (1920–2016), to become one of the early specialists on the Dead Sea Scrolls and a world expert in Aramaic, the native language of Jesus. Fitzmyer would be elected president of the Catholic Biblical Association (1969–70), president of the Society of Biblical Literature (1979), and president of the Studiorum Novi Testamenti Societas (1992–93). So far, he has been the only American Jesuit to be appointed a member of the Pontifical Biblical Commission (1984–95); he proved influential in drafting its acclaimed document *The Interpretation of the Bible in the Church* (1993).

A widely used *Introductory Bibliography for the Study of Scripture* (1961) was coauthored by Fitzmyer and Glanzman. After a licentiate (master's degree) at the Biblicum, Glanzman began research with Albright at Johns Hopkins but never finished his dissertation.[28] Suffering from writer's block, he proved, nevertheless, a highly effective biblical teacher at Woodstock College (1953–62) and Fordham University (1962–76). His contemporary, Frederick Moriarty, SJ (1913–2004), while more prolific in publications, also excelled as a teacher of the Old Testament. After a master's degree under Albright at Johns Hopkins (1947), Moriarty received a licentiate at the Biblicum (1949). He taught for many years at Weston College, Boston College, and the Gregorian University. We (Kendall and O'Collins) remain lastingly grateful to him for bringing us together over a doctoral dissertation in 1973, and so enabling such joint publications as our "The Uniqueness of the Easter Appearances," *CBQ* 54 (1992): 287–307.

Eventually Jesuits and other Catholic scriptural scholars became collaborators with Albright, notably in a series he initiated, the Anchor Bible Commentary. Brown set a high standard for the NT commentaries by his two volumes on the Fourth Gospel, followed later by a separate volume on the Letters of John. After Albright's death, Fitzmyer maintained the academic rigor of Brown, with commentaries on Luke (1981), Romans (1993), the Acts of the Apostles (1998), and First Corinthians (2008). Dahood had already published the three-volume *Psalms* (1966–70) for the OT section of the Anchor Bible. But we are getting ahead of ourselves. We should return to the 1950s and describe the growing Jesuit input in the biblical movement.

During that period two Jesuit OT scholars, the Canadian Roderick A. F. MacKenzie (1911–94) and the American John L. McKenzie (1910–91), made significant impacts on biblical interpretation, in particular in critical history. In 1962, the former would become for six years rector of the Pontifical Biblical Institute, Rome, and prove influential during the Second Vatican Council.[29] The latter wrote a work on the OT embodying new developments in Catholic biblical scholarship and intended for a general readership: *The Two-Edged Sword: An Interpretation of the Old Testament* (1953). The book introduced many Catholics and other Christians to a new world of scholarship. His subsequent *A Dictionary of the Bible* (1965) enjoyed enormous popularity and remains in use.

The large, mainly Protestant organization, the Society of Biblical Literature, showed its esteem for John McKenzie by electing him president in 1966 and thus making him the first Catholic to be their president.

From the 1950s into the 1960s, fresh opposition to critical biblical scholarship had flared up, both in the United States and Rome (especially at the Lateran University). The 1950 encyclical *Humani Generis* was aimed primarily against the *Nouvelle Théologie* of Yves Congar, OP, Henri de Lubac, SJ, and others, but its nervous warnings also touched the historical nature of Genesis 1—11 and, in particular, Genesis 1—3. These warnings about human origins had repercussions for Pauline scholars. How could they harmonize scientific hypotheses about polygenism with the classic doctrine of original sin stemming from Romans 5:12–21? The editor of the *American Ecclesiastical Review*, Joseph Clifford Fenton, after attacking John Courtney Murray over religious liberty, turned to virulent criticism of the biblical movement. Here he was supported by a powerful friend who from 1958 to 1967 served as the apostolic delegate in the United States, Egidio Vagnozzi (1906–80; created cardinal in 1967).[30]

VATICAN II AND BEYOND

Earlier we recalled that there was only one Jesuit from the United States (John Courtney Murray) appointed a *peritus* at the Second Vatican Council, and Murray was not a biblical specialist. The biblical *periti* at Vatican II included the Canadian Roderick MacKenzie, SJ, some American exegetes who were not Jesuits (e.g., Barnabas Ahern, CP, Eugene H. Maly, and John E. Steinmueller), and a number of European Scripture scholars who again were not Jesuits (e.g., Pierre Benoit, OP, and Beda Rigaux, OFM). Nevertheless, American Jesuit biblical scholars had their influence at the Council.

In 1959, the rector of the Pontifical Biblical Institute, a German-speaking Swiss Jesuit, Ernst Vogt, submitted, on his own behalf and on behalf of eighteen other professors of the Biblicum, a petition to a preparatory commission of Vatican II. They asked that the Council address the scandal of anti-Semitism and clarify scriptural texts often wrongly used against Jews. The nineteen included notable American Jesuits: Mitchell Dahood, Robert Dyson, Francis McCool, and William Moran.[31] In the event, Vatican II devoted some new teaching to these questions (*Lumen Gentium* 16 and *Nostra Aetate* 4) and, under the leadership of John XXIII and Cardinal Bea, inaugurated a happier era in the Church's openness to Judaism. Beyond question, other groups and individuals played a major part in changing Catholic teaching and practice vis-à-vis Jews. But the cause was dear to Americans on the staff of the PBI, and they too helped bring it to fruition.[32]

Before the Council and during its opening session, the Biblicum itself had come under fire. Two American professors, Robert Dyson and Robert North, were accused of espousing the misguided methods of "liberal Protestantism" and harming Catholic doctrine on OT revelation.[33] These attacks (often anonymous), coming from Antonino Romeo of the Lateran University, ceased for a while. Then, on the eve of Vatican II, a former student of Romeo, Francesco Spadafora, published a pamphlet that accused Stanislaus Lyonnet, SJ, the dean of the Biblicum, and Maximilian Zerwick, SJ, of denying the historicity of the Gospels. In the summer of 1962, a few months before John XXIII opened the Council, they were removed from their teaching posts but were eventually rehabilitated in the spring of 1964. Curiously, Lyonnet remained dean during those two years, even though he was prohibited from teaching.[34] The saga of Lyonnet and Zerwick had a special American connection, as, along with some other Europeans, both were members of the CBA.

The Canadian rector, Roderick MacKenzie, and several American Jesuit professors of the Biblicum staged a dramatic defense of critical scholarship and its importance for the Church's teaching office and theology. They did this on November 21, 1962, the very day that John XXIII withdrew the first schema on the sources of revelation and entrusted its revision to a special commission presided over by (a) Cardinal Alfredo Ottaviani (1890–1979), the secretary of the Holy Office (from 1959–66, and then its pro-prefect until 1968), and (b) Cardinal Augustin Bea, a former rector of the Biblicum and now president (1960–68) of the new Secretariat for the Promotion of Christian Unity. (Ottaviani was known to be a friend of Fenton and a firm opponent of John Courtney Murray.) On the afternoon of November 21, a

German Jesuit, Norbert Lohfink, defended a thesis on Deuteronomy written under the direction of the American Jesuit William L. Moran (1921–2000). The defense was attended by twelve cardinals, 150 bishops, and numerous others connected with the first session of Vatican II (October–December 1962).[35] The occasion became a major exhibition of the scholarly standards of the Biblicum and the importance of biblical learning for the whole Church.

Moran (at the Biblicum 1958–66) made significant contributions to scriptural scholarship. In 1966, he became professor of Assyriology at Harvard, leaving the Jesuit Order three years later. He is noted for his definitive *Amarna Letters*, published by Johns Hopkins Press in 1992. Robert A. Di Vito (b. 1949), who did his Harvard PhD under Moran, published several perceptive articles, was involved in the revision of the OT section of the New American Bible (see below), and became renowned as an excellent teacher at Loyola University, Chicago (1991–). Leaving the Society of Jesus as an ordained priest, Di Vito taught appreciative young Jesuits, among many others. Three other acclaimed biblical scholars left the Society of Jesus prior to being ordained priests. After receiving his PhD from Harvard, Eugene C. Ulrich (b. 1938) was appointed John A. O'Brien Professor of Theology at the University of Notre Dame. He has specialized in the Hebrew Scriptures, the Dead Sea Scrolls, and the Septuagint. With Oxford University Press, he has published five volumes of the critical edition of the Dead Sea Scrolls, *Discoveries in the Judean Desert*. After a PhD at Harvard, John ("Jack") Miles (b. 1942) became an editor for Doubleday and the University of California Press. He won a Pulitzer Prize in biography for his 1995 book, *God: A Biography*. After receiving a PhD from Harvard, Michael Coogan (b. 1942) became a lecturer on the Hebrew Bible at Harvard Divinity School, director of publications for the Harvard Semitic Museum, and editor in chief of Oxford Biblical Studies Online. Among ex-Jesuits who are deceased, we should not forget Anthony ("Tony") J. Saldarini (1941–2001). He received his PhD in Near Eastern languages at Yale (1971), became a noted and widely published expert on the Jewish background to the NT, and taught for over twenty-five years at Boston College.

POST–VATICAN II

To what extent have Jesuit biblical scholars in the United States succeeded in encouraging theologians to make the study of the Scriptures "the very soul" of their work? We still seem some distance from that happening. Nowadays we are blessed by many admirable commentaries on the Gospels and other NT books, studies of St. Paul, scripturally based examinations of the early Church's faith and life, and biblical dictionaries. But almost the last book you could expect to find on the desk of *many* English-speaking theologians (fundamental, systematic, or moral) would be the *New Jerome Biblical Commentary* or *The New Interpreter's Dictionary of the Bible*, not to speak of Joel Marcus's two volumes on Mark's Gospel, James Dunn on Paul, or Larry Hurtado on devotion to Jesus in early Christianity. On the desk of Catholic theologians, you will generally find a translation of the entire Bible and perhaps a copy of the Greek New Testament. But many of them still expect to pass straight from the scriptural text to theological reflections and conclusions while largely ignoring what biblical experts have to say.

In 1997, we (Kendall and O'Collins) published *The Bible for Theology*,[36] hoping to help effect a change. O'Collins returned to this issue in 2018, with a chapter ("Ten Principles for Theologians Interpreting the Scriptures") in his *Inspiration: Towards a Christian Interpretation of Biblical Interpretation*.[37] But it still remains a big task to persuade many theologians to take on board the best insights from contemporary biblical scholars, not to mention the treasures found in the reception of the inspired Scriptures during the whole history of Christianity.[38] Apropos of the latter, you are unlikely to find in the library of theologians such works as *The Oxford Handbook of the Reception History of the Bible* (2011), the four volumes of *The Cambridge History of the Bible* (2012), and (by the end of 2017) the fifteen volumes of de Gruyter's *Encyclopedia of the Bible and Its Reception* (2009–).

Jesuit and other scriptural scholars in the United States and elsewhere have, however, succeeded in promoting serious attention to biblical research in the fields of catechetics and spiritual theology. In fact, Fitzmyer moved into the first, with his highly successful *A Christological Catechism: New Testament Answers* (1982). He contributed to the second field with his *Spiritual Exercises Based on Paul's Epistle to the*

Romans (1995). David Stanley produced *A Modern Scriptural Approach to the Spiritual Exercises* (1967), *The Spiritual Exercises with the Gospel of St. John* (1986), and a notable article in *Theological Studies* for 1968, "Contemplation of the Gospels, Ignatius Loyola, and the Contemporary Christian" (417–43).

Nowadays those who are specialists in providing catechetical material normally do their best to mediate insightful and life-giving insights from biblical scholarship. Likewise, those who have led work in Ignatian spirituality (to whom we will turn in chap. 6) have been shining examples in taking on board biblical scholarship to illuminate and deepen their understanding of the Spiritual Exercises. Some Jesuit scriptural experts in the United States (e.g., Clifford and Harrington) have furthered this development, as did Cardinal Martini (rector of the Biblicum 1969–78) in his biblically based versions of the Spiritual Exercises (e.g., the Exercises shaped by one or other of the four Evangelists).

A Bostonian, Daniel Harrington, symbolized the ideals of American Jesuit contributions to biblical scholarship during the post–Vatican II period. We saw above how for over forty years he edited the invaluable *New Testament Abstracts*. He was also editor of the eighteen-volume *Sacra Pagina* commentaries on the books of the New Testament published by Liturgical Press (Collegeville, MN). For *America* magazine, he wrote a regular scriptural column and never abandoned the project of mediating to a wider public the insights of the best biblical scholars. With this aim he also published such books as *Mediating Paul Today* (2008). A vivid and affectionate article by James Martin, SJ, in *America* (February 8, 2017) illustrates how Harrington combined a critical mind with the eyes of faith. Harrington used his rich talents to do nothing less than promote "sacred scripture in the life of the Church," the theme of an outstanding chapter from Vatican II (*DV* 21–26).

Shortly after the Catholic Biblical Association came into existence in 1936, its members decided to produce a new translation of the Bible. Their version of the NT was published in 1941 and for decades widely used by American Catholics. When the OT version finally appeared in 1970, the New American Bible (NAB) version was complete. It came to be read during the liturgy of many churches, in the United States and beyond. Seven Jesuits collaborated in the preparation of the OT translation. Three of them have been mentioned above: Collins, Roderick MacKenzie, and Moriarty.

However, liturgical and private use revealed defects in the NAB, and, less than eight years after its publication, new editorial boards were established to prepare a revision. The chairman of the board for revising the NT was an American Jesuit, Francis T. Gignac (1933–2014). He had taken his DPhil at the University of Oxford and was a professor at the Catholic University of America (1974–2013). He deserves major credit for carrying through the 1986 revision of the NT, commonly regarded as a huge improvement over the first version and approved in the same year by the U.S. bishops. Gignac's translation committee ("revisers") included two other Jesuits: C. Homer Giblin (1929–2002), who had taken his doctorate at the Biblicum and taught for years at Fordham University, and John R. Keating (b. 1930), who taught at Fordham University, the Jesuit School of Theology, Berkeley, and Georgetown University.[39]

Five Jesuits (including Clifford, Fitzmyer, Gignac, and Harrington) belonged to the group of editors and "revisers" who updated all but one of the OT books for the NAB and finished their task in 2010. The U.S. bishops had mandated a psalter that used inclusive language, spelled out appropriate criteria for the translation, and approved these criteria by a vote of 84 percent in favor. A separate board of editors, with Richard Clifford the only Jesuit among them, worked for over two years to produce in 1991 an excellent translation of the Psalms, which was incorporated in the NAB. But the machinations of several Jesuits resident in Rome and the United States saw to it that the Vatican's Congregation for the Doctrine of the Faith never approved the inclusive Psalter.[40] When the entire revised NAB was published in 2011 as NABRE, it contained the 1986 revised NT and the fully revised OT, except for a less inclusive Psalter (2010) that replaced the one that had been produced by Clifford and the other scholars in 1991 and widely used until 1996.

Colleagues in biblical studies recognized what American Jesuits achieved. From 1971 to 1976, Fitzmyer served as editor of the *Journal of Biblical Literature*—the only Jesuit so far to have done so. Clifford was editor of *Catholic Biblical Quarterly* (1976–79)—the second Jesuit to have held the role after Michael Gruenthaner (see above). Fitzmyer served as editor for the *CBQ* from 1980 to 1984.

An ecumenical involvement, practiced by American (and other) Jesuit biblical scholars, has continued. James Swetnam, SJ (b. 1928), took his DPhil at Oxford University and taught at the Biblicum for fifty years. John Donahue, SJ (b. 1933), received his PhD from the Divinity School of the University of Chicago and went on to become an authority on the parables of Jesus. William J. Fulco, SJ (b. 1936), after his PhD from Yale in Near Eastern languages and literature, became a celebrated biblical teacher and archaeologist. He worked with Mel Gibson in producing a text in Aramaic and Latin for the 2004 film *The Passion of the Christ*. Jerome H. Neyrey, SJ (b. 1940), earned his PhD at Yale and became a leading exponent of a sociological approach to scriptural studies. Robert Wild, SJ (b. 1940), received his PhD at Harvard and was an acclaimed biblical scholar, before being appointed president of Weston Jesuit School of Theology (from 1992) and then president of Marquette University (from 1996). Thomas H. Tobin, SJ (b. 1945), was awarded his PhD at Harvard, became a recognized expert on the New Testament and Philo, and has spent his teaching life at Loyola University, Chicago. John C. Endres, SJ (b. 1946), earned his PhD at Vanderbilt and taught for many years at the Jesuit School of Theology Berkeley. The current dean of the Boston College School of Theology and Ministry is Thomas D. Stegman, SJ, an outstanding teacher and scholar, who took his doctorate (in Pauline studies) at Candler School of Theology, Emory University. One of Stegman's colleagues at Boston College is Michael R. Simone, SJ (PhD from Johns Hopkins). American Jesuits now teaching at the Biblicum include Dean P. Béchard (PhD from Yale) and Anthony P. SooHoo (PhD from New York University).

Béchard and SooHoo remind us that American Jesuit biblical scholars continue to make their contribution both in the United States *and in Rome*. We have already seen other examples. Further examples would include—the list is not exclusive—Dennis J. McCarthy (1924–83) and John Kilgallen (1934–2019), both at the Biblicum, Dennis M. Hamm (b. 1936, at Creighton University, Omaha), William S. Kurz (b. 1939, at Marquette University), Anthony Forte (b. 1951, at the Biblicum), and Scott N. Brodeur (b. 1957, at the Gregorian).

A major publishing event of 2018 was the appearance of *The Paulist Biblical Commentary*. Two of the six editors (Clifford and Stegman) and twelve of the seventy-five contributors were Jesuits. Their contribution to biblical studies remains vibrant. To be sure, the numbers of young men entering the Society of Jesus in the 1940s and 1950s produced correspondingly large numbers of biblical scholars for a golden age of biblical scholars. Their successors are fewer, but still worthy. Add, too, that across the United States many talented and well-prepared lay scholars teach the Scriptures at Jesuit universities and colleges. Through these women and men, whose research was often supervised by Jesuits, the Jesuit contribution to biblical studies also continues.

CHAPTER 6

IGNATIAN SPIRITUALITY

IN THE MID-1980S a Russian Orthodox bishop, president of a theological academy in Moscow, visited the Gregorian University in Rome to check courses and consider further collaboration. He was pleasantly surprised to find that there was no officially prescribed philosophy and that the Gregorian offered courses and seminars in analytic, Aristotelian, existentialist, idealist, Marxist, Thomist, and other forms of philosophy. He was not so happy to find that the university had an institute of spirituality, which was quite distinct from the theology faculty. "Shouldn't all theology be spiritual?" he asked.[1] Ideally, the archbishop was correct. But in an imperfect world we often have to tolerate an organizational separation between theology and spirituality, hoping (a) that courses and publications in spirituality will be well founded in the Scriptures, doctrine, and historical research and (b) that work in theology will be open to and nourish Christian spiritual life.

Christian spirituality can be described as the systematic practice of and reflection on a devout and disciplined following of Jesus. Spirituality has always called for an ascetical and prayerful life in which a spiritual guide and the light of the Holy Spirit help discern the direction in which individuals and communities are being led (1 Thess 5:19–22; 1 John 4:1). Schools or styles of spirituality have often matched the charisms of such orders as the Benedictines, Carmelites, Carthusians, Dominicans, Franciscans, and Jesuits. As a field of study, spirituality involves theological (including liturgical), scriptural, historical, psychological, and social elements. Eastern theology differs from Western through the primacy it assigns to the Spirit and, consequently, to Christian spirituality and life. Spirituality is viewed as theology "from within." Thus, one can understand the unease of the Russian bishop at the separation of spirituality and theology in the Gregorian's program of studies.

The *Dictionnaire de Spiritualité* (published from 1932 to 1995 in twenty-one volumes) splendidly exemplifies what can be expected from a biblical, doctrinal, and historical spirituality.[2] Founded by French Jesuits, it eventually contained nine thousand entries. Its more than sixteen hundred contributors included such American Jesuits as Joseph Fitzmyer (one article), Francis A. Sullivan (two articles), Gustave Weigel (one article), and Jared Wicks (nine articles). As we might say, Fitzmyer represents biblical spirituality, Sullivan and Weigel represent doctrinal spirituality, and Wicks represents historical spirituality. But what was the background to the emergence of modern spirituality and, in particular, the Jesuit development of spirituality, specifically Ignatian spirituality, in the United States?

FROM JOHN CARROLL TO VATICAN II

Chapter 1 showed what Archbishop John Carroll did toward encouraging devotion to the Sacred Heart of Jesus and the Blessed Virgin Mary.[3] He also encouraged the printing in Philadelphia of the Douay-Rheims Bible, the first Catholic Bible published in the United States (1790). Many Catholic households had a copy of this Bible, even if relatively few used it for prayer and reflection.

Jesuits at Georgetown University and Woodstock College, after its foundation in 1869, encouraged devotion to the Sacred Heart, especially through publishing the widely distributed *Messenger of the Sacred Heart*. For many decades, Jesuits promoted popular spirituality. They spread devotion to the Sacred Heart through the Apostleship of Prayer and used parish missions to establish Confraternities of the Apostleship of Prayer. As we saw in chapter 1, two Jesuits, Francis Finn and Henry Spalding, published numerous books of edifying fiction, a form of practical spirituality that inculcated appropriate Christian behavior.

In chapters 1 and 4, we recalled how Daniel Lord, SJ, and John

LaFarge, SJ, launched the Institute of Social Order; its journal, *Social Order*, continued to be published until 1963. In applying the teaching of Leo XIII and Pius XI to the American scene, they developed a social spirituality for the working classes. LaFarge's agenda included campaigning for civil rights, interracial justice, and an end to social barriers in the Catholic Church. His best-selling autobiography, *The Manner Is Ordinary* (1954), shared with a wide public the way he lived Jesuit spirituality. As national director of the Sodality of the Blessed Virgin Mary (1925–48), Lord shaped its magazine, *The Queen's Work*, into an effective aid for the spirituality of young people.

Three wider developments in Catholic Christianity provided the ground out of which a new Ignatian, rather than a largely Jesuit, spirituality grew and flourished. First, the 1943 encyclical of Pius XII, *Divino Afflante Spiritu*, in the drafting of which the rector of the Biblicum, Augustin (later Cardinal) Bea, played a significant role, encouraged Catholic scriptural scholars to accept and practice the best of modern biblical criticism. Chapter 5 described the flowering of American biblical scholarship, which through its publications and teaching provided spiritual experts and others with material from the four Gospels, Paul, Isaiah, and other inspired texts. That same chapter also noted how some Jesuit biblical scholars (Joseph Fitzmyer, Daniel Harrington, Carlo Maria Martini, and David Stanley) directly applied their scriptural expertise to spirituality by writing such books as the *Spiritual Exercises Based on Paul's Epistle to the Romans* (Fitzmyer, 1995).

The rich development of American Jesuit spirituality could never have happened without the sources and resources made available by biblical experts. Unless a Christian spirituality is biblically based, it will lack depth and richness. In its Constitution on Divine Revelation (*Dei Verbum*) the Second Vatican Council (1962–65) described the Scriptures as a "pure and lasting fountain of the spiritual life" (art. 21). The same constitution prescribed constant reading and praying over the inspired texts (art. 25).[4] Many publications were to show biblical insights shaping the contributions coming from leaders in spirituality: for instance, *Seek My Face: Prayer as Personal Relationship in Scripture* (2nd ed., 2009) by William A. Barry, SJ (b. 1930). The biblical movement also had a major influence on liturgical reforms introduced by Vatican II: for instance, a richer selection of scriptural readings for the Divine Office and a much wider representation of the Scriptures in the revised lectionary (*Sacrosanctum Concilium* 51, 92).

Second, unlike modern biblical scholarship, the liturgical movement started among Catholics and soon spread to other Christian communities. It encouraged all members of the Church to participate actively in official worship and let the Eucharist become the real center of their community and personal life. The movement was initiated by Abbot Prosper Guéranger (1805–75) and the Benedictine Abbey of Solesmes. Official encouragement came in 1903 when Pius X legislated measures encouraging frequent communion and effecting the reform of Church music. Across Europe, Benedictines such as Lambert Beauduin (1873–1960) and Odo Casel (1896–1948), with others like Pius Parsch (1884–1954), Romano Guardini (1885–1968), and Josef Jungmann, SJ (1889–1975), promoted not only scholarly studies of the liturgy but also its pastoral development. Pius XII's 1947 encyclical, *Mediator Dei*, brought certain reforms, which culminated in the restoration of the Holy Week ceremonies.

In the United States, some Benedictines like Virgil G. Michel (1890–1938) and his more famous assistant, Godfrey L. Diekmann (1908–2002), dedicated themselves to the liturgical movement. In the 1940s and 1950s, Diekmann was a key figure in the movement and would become a frequent lecturer for the summer school at the Jesuit University of San Francisco; he was also a *peritus* at the Second Vatican Council. But, as the liturgical movement took hold in the United States, often lay activists rather than members of monastic communities played key roles.[5]

Gerald Ellard, SJ (1884–1963), worked with Benedictines and others in founding *Orate Fratres* (1926), which was eventually renamed *Worship*. When Ellard died suddenly in 1963, the journal carried warm tributes to his work in promoting liturgical renewal.[6] Over the years he had contributed fifty-four main articles and numerous book reviews, and he published several books, including the best-selling *Christian Life and Worship* (1940).[7] He helped to dispel the myth of Jesuits being antiliturgical. To be sure, Ignatius Loyola expected "the Creator to work directly" on those making the Spiritual Exercises (Annotation 15). But such heart-to-heart communing with God did not dispense with the sacraments and the Divine Office. Ignatius expected retreatants to attend Mass and Vespers each day (Annotation 20). A spirituality, whether Ignatian or otherwise, that declines to incorporate the sacraments and, in some measure, the Divine Office cannot claim to be truly Catholic.

Ressourcement theology, or a theology that returns to the sources, formed a third movement that empowered the growth of Ignatian spirituality in the United States.[8] This theology, developed by such French theologians as Yves Congar, OP, Jean Daniélou, SJ, and Henri de Lubac, SJ, used a "genetic" method, a return to the sources that studied first the biblical witness and then the subsequent history of doctrinal development. By starting from the Scriptures and the fathers, it tracked, along the lines of John Henry Newman's view of doctrinal development, the living tradition and what it embodied for growth and change in Church teaching and practice.

In its Decree on the Appropriate Renewal of Religious Life (*Perfectae Caritatis*), Vatican II was to stress not only "adaptation to the changed conditions of our time" but also *ressourcement*: "the constant return to the sources of all Christian life and to the original spirit of the [religious] institutes" (art. 2). In this decree the role of *ressourcement* comes constantly into view. Apropos of the prayer life of religious men and women, *Perfectae Caritatis* recommends that they should draw from "the authentic sources of Christian spirituality." That means drawing not only from the Eucharist but also from daily contact with "the Holy Scripture in order that, by reading and meditating on Holy Writ, they may learn 'the surpassing worth of knowing Jesus Christ' (Phil. 3:8)" (art. 6). The return to the sources also involves faithfully recognizing and observing "their founders' spirit and special aims...as well as their sound traditions—all of which make up the patrimony of each institute" (art. 2).

Through a *ressourcement* approach, Ignatian spirituality was blessed by the work of Ignacio Iparraguire, SJ (1911–73).[9] His thesis at the Gregorian University, *The Practice of the Exercises of St Ignatius during the Life of the Author*, became the first volume in a trilogy on the history of the Spiritual Exercises. As well as teaching at the Gregorian, Iparraguire helped to set up the Centrum Ignatianum Spiritualitatis (CIS) at the Jesuit headquarters in Rome. Besides offering courses and lectures, this center produced from 1970 to 2011 the *Review of Ignatian Spirituality*, which attended to the interpretation and practice of the Spiritual Exercises. Iparraguire encouraged adapting the Exercises to the personal situation of the retreatants, contributed to the greater popularity of individually directed retreats, and persuaded many Jesuits (and others) of the need to form competent directors.

In the aftermath of World War II, the rediscovery of the historical sources of Jesuit identity led to the creation of specialist journals in spirituality. In France, Maurice Giuliani, SJ, founded in 1954 a revue of spiritual formation, *Christus*. In England, James Walsh, SJ, founded in 1961 a similar journal, *The Way*. They joined an existing stable of journals in Germany, Spain, and France. The bimonthly review *Geist und Leben: Zeitschrift für Spiritualität* was founded by German Jesuits in 1926 as *Zeitschrift für Aszese und Mystik* (renamed *Geist und Leben* in 1947) and shaped by Friedrich Wulf, SJ, editor from 1947 to 1989 and a *peritus* at the Second Vatican Council. A Dominican, J. G. Arintero, founded the Spanish review *La vida sobrenatural* in 1921, whereas a Jesuit, Joseph de Guibert, founded the *Revue d'ascetique et de mystique* in 1920. He went on to become one of the three Jesuit scholars from Toulouse who initiated the *Dictionnaire de Spiritualité*.

GOLDEN YEARS IN THE UNITED STATES

Review for Religious, founded and published by Jesuits of the Missouri Province (from 1942 to 2012), was read by men and women religious around the world, whether members of active, apostolic institutes or contemplative monastic communities. In its post–Vatican II years, the review was edited for over twenty years (1988–2010) by David L. Fleming, SJ (1934–2011). Through *Draw Me into Your Friendship* (1996), a literal translation and contemporary reading of St. Ignatius's *Spiritual Exercises*, Fleming provided an invaluable resource both for those doing the Exercises and those directing them. Earlier he had selected the best articles that had appeared in *Review for Religious* to produce *Notes on the Spiritual Exercises of St. Ignatius of Loyola* (1981). Both of us (Kendall and O'Collins) remain lastingly grateful to Fleming for the advice he gave when we were preparing for publication *Seek God Everywhere*, reflections on the Spiritual Exercises by Anthony de Mello, SJ (1931–87).[10]

In 1951, Louis J. Puhl, SJ, published with Loyola Press (Chicago) *The Spiritual Exercises of St. Ignatius*, an English translation made in the light of studies of the original manuscripts. This became for decades the standard English translation and was used around the world by de Mello and innumerable others. The translations by Fleming and by two English Jesuits, Joseph A. Munitiz and Philip Endean (1996; updated 2004), have supplanted that by Puhl.

Historical studies and contemporary experience prompted a rediscovery (*ressourcement*) of the importance of doing the Spiritual Exercises by way of an individually guided retreat lasting up to thirty days. American Jesuit leaders in this development supplied help for those doing the Exercises and for those directing them. One can recall, for instance, George A. Aschenbrenner (b. 1932), *Stretched for Greater Glory: What to Expect from the Spiritual Exercises* (2004); William Barry, *Allowing the Creator to Deal with the Creature: An Approach to the Spiritual Exercises of Ignatius of Loyola* (1994); John C. Futrell (1927–2008) with Marian Cowan, CSJ, *Companions in Grace: A Handbook for Directors of the Exercises* (2000).

American Jesuits have continued to write numerous works on the Exercises. James J. Martin (b. 1960) put out the first-ever e-retreat: *Together on Retreat: Meeting Jesus in Prayer* (2013). A few years earlier he had achieved another "first" with *The Jesuit Guide to (Almost) Everything*, the first general introduction to Jesuit spirituality from a mainstream publishing house (revised and updated, New York: Harper One, 2009).

Some of the American specialists also published studies of practices that St. Ignatius proposed for those making the Exercises: for instance, the rules for the discernment of spirits (*Spiritual Exercises*, 314–36). God is identified as the fundamental "good spirit"; "the enemy of our human nature" is identified as "Satan," the dominant "evil spirit" (*SpEx*, 136–42, 322). The good spirits characteristically give "encouragement, strength, and consolation," whereas the evil spirits produce sadness and anxiety, always attempting to block progress in the following of Christ (*SpEx*, 315).[11] Jules J. Toner, SJ, published a guide for identifying the spirits affecting those making the Exercises: *A Commentary on Saint Ignatius' Rules for the Discernment of Spirits* (1982). In volume 2 of *Studies in the Spirituality of Jesuits*, Futrell had already published *Ignatian Discernment* (April 1970).

Another practice inculcated by the Exercises was the examen, a prayer that checks whether one is moving ahead or slipping back in the service of God. This practice could lead retreatants into one-sidedly looking for sin, rather than becoming aware of the way God had been gifting them during the period under review. In a significant 1972 article for the *Review for Religious*, Aschenbrenner proposed a "consciousness" examen rather than an examination of conscience. In 2007, he spelled out this proposal in a book, *Consciousness Examen*[12] (Chicago: Loyola Press).

Besides illuminating the Exercises for retreatants themselves, Aschenbrenner, Barry, Fleming, and other American Jesuits helped those who directed the Spiritual Exercises by offering courses and publications that recovered Ignatius's advice to allow "the Creator to work directly with the creature and the creature with the Creator and Lord" (Annotations, 15). Ignatius wanted directors to be excellent listeners who could adapt the Exercises to the needs of their directees and help them discover the presence of God in their prayer and lives. Barry and William J. Connolly, SJ (1925–2013), published *The Practice of Spiritual Direction* (1982), and Fleming put out *The Christian Ministry of Spiritual Direction* (1988). *The Practice of Spiritual Direction* was translated into fourteen other languages, which included all the major European languages, Chinese (two different translations), Korean, and Vietnamese.

The Center for Religious Development (CRD), established in 1971 by Barry, Connolly, and four other Jesuits in Cambridge, Massachusetts, trained spiritual directors for many years until it closed in 2009. The staff of CRD were at the heart of the renewal in the Spiritual Exercises. They enlisted and instructed others in the delicate ministry not only of directing the Exercises but also of guiding people in living seriously their commitment to Jesus Christ.[13] A strong emphasis on individual spiritual direction as an overarching goal for Jesuits in the United States is now enshrined as a "Universal Apostolic Preference." CRD has had a worldwide impact through the translations of *The Practice of Spiritual Direction* and through graduates of its programs training spiritual directors in the United States and other countries. Some graduates of CRD helped found Spiritual Directors International.

Spirituality and retreat centers form a latter-day counterpart to the Benedictine monastery at Montserrat and the cave at Manresa, where Ignatius meditated, contemplated, and began to compose the first text of the *Spiritual Exercises* and give fuller shape to what is known as Ignatian spirituality. Nowadays retreat houses offer directed retreats of five, eight, or thirty days, as well as traditional "preached" retreats. Such houses include Eastern Point Retreat House (Gloucester, Massachusetts)[14] along with similar centers in the United States and abroad (for instance, Loyola House in Guelph, Ontario, and St Beuno's spirituality center in Wales). Such Jesuit colleges and universities as Boston College, Creighton University, Loyola Marymount University, and

Marquette University offer resources for promoting Ignatian spirituality among students, staff, and faculty members. Many Jesuit parishes and centers also offer directors for "the retreat in daily life," a popular and fruitful way of doing the Exercises that Ignatius himself had recommended (Annotations 19).[15]

An East Coast Jesuit, George Maloney (1924–2005), wrote on the Spiritual Exercises. But it was what he had to say on Eastern Christian spirituality that won him many readers. Books like *Russian Hesychasm* (1973), *Inward Stillness* (1975), *Prayer of the Heart* (1981), and *Pilgrimage of the Heart* (1983) made him the leading Jesuit interpreter of Eastern spirituality in his generation. He served as editor of *Diakonia*, a journal of the John XXIII center (New York City) devoted to Eastern Christian studies.

After founding the *Review for Religious*, in 1961 the Missouri Province opened in St. Louis the Institute of Jesuit Sources, with the commission to publish texts and studies not only in Jesuit spirituality but also in Jesuit history and pedagogy. The institute published translations of Jesuit primary sources, such as early directories for giving the Exercises, letters, and other writings of Ignatius and his first companions, and the *Constitutions of the Society of Jesus and Their Complementary Norms*. From September 1969, the institute issued *Studies in the Spirituality of Jesuits*; the series continues today.

The Institute of Jesuit Sources enjoyed excellent historians as its directors: George E. Ganss, SJ (1905–2000), and John W. Padberg, SJ (b. 1926). The founding director and editor, Ganss, served until 1986, when Padberg took over until 2014. That was the year when the Institute of Jesuit Sources moved to Boston and was subsumed under the newly founded Institute for Advanced Jesuit Studies at Boston College. This institute, as well as publishing *Studies in the Spirituality of Jesuits*, sponsors a quarterly, the *Journal of Jesuit Studies* (2014–), and offers lectures, workshops, and summer courses in Jesuit history and Ignatian spirituality.[16]

VISITING JESUITS

Any account of the Jesuit contributions to spirituality in the United States would be incomplete if it ignored such visiting Jesuits as Pierre Teilhard de Chardin (1881–1955), Anthony de Mello, James Walsh (1920–86), and Pope Francis (b. 1936).

(1) The spiritual influence of Teilhard de Chardin in the United States was largely posthumous. Having visited the United States before the Second World War, he returned toward the end of his life and lived in a Jesuit residence in New York, where he died on Easter Sunday 1955. It was only then that his spiritual classics began to appear in French and then English: *The Phenomenon of Man* (1959), *The Divine Milieu* (1960), and other works. A priest-paleontologist, famous for his role in the discovery of the Peking Man, Teilhard embodied a harmony between science and faith and preached the value of human activity and the material universe in the ongoing "christification" of the universe. Raymond Schroth, SJ (b. 1933), describes vividly how this "patron 'saint' of the French spirit infused the American church."[17]

(2) In 1973 de Mello founded near Pune, India, the Sadhana ("Way to God") Institute, a center for training spiritual guides and directors of retreats. An acclaimed spiritual master, he often lectured in the United States—for instance, during the summer programs at the University of San Francisco. He also published several best-selling spiritual works with Doubleday (New York): for example, *Song of the Bird*; *Sadhana: A Way to God*; and *Wellsprings: A Book of Spiritual Exercises*.

(3) Walsh came from England and made his contribution to the USF summer schools—not least through being a resource person for the thirty-day retreats that some of the students did over their summer break at Los Altos, California.

(4) *Theological Studies* took time before featuring major documents and pastoral themes from Pope Francis. The first article on him came three years after his election as pope and was written by an Argentinian Jesuit: Juan Carlos Scannone, "Pope Francis and the Theology of the People."[18]

The second issue of *Theological Studies* for 2016 contained eight articles on Francis's encyclical concerned with the state and future of our planet, *Laudato Si'*, with one of the articles ("A Pauline Complement to *Laudato Si'*") coming from the Australian NT scholar, Brendan Byrne, SJ. *Theological Studies* was to revisit *Laudato Si'* with three articles dedicated to the encyclical in the June issue of 2018.

The final issue of *Theological Studies* for 2016 included an article by O'Collins: "The Joy of Love (*Amoris Laetitia*): The Papal Exhortation in Its Context."[19] In 2017, *Theological Studies* published four articles on the teaching of Pope Francis. James F. Keenan, SJ, examined the reception of *Amoris Laetitia*.[20] The other three articles were not written by Jesuits: the first provided an Indian perspective on *Laudato Si'*; a related article took up ecology as ecclesiology. The third article reflected on the Eucharist in the context of the global refugee crisis. It cited the Mass celebrated by Pope Francis on the island of Lampedusa (July 13, 2013); the pope used a wooden chalice fashioned from the driftwood of a refugee shipwreck. In 2018 *Theological Studies* continued to pay attention to *Amoris Laetitia*, with an article by Todd A. Salzman and Michael G. Lawler, "*Amoris Laetitia*: Towards an Anthropological and Methodological Integration of Catholic Social and Sexual Ethics."

What prominence did other Jesuit publications give to Pope Francis and his teaching? Given the strong spiritual and pastoral nature of the pope's messages, he was taken up quickly by *Studies in the Spirituality of Jesuits*. In 2013, its autumn and winter issues published *Writings on Jesuit Spirituality* that came from Francis before he had been elected pope and illuminated the background to his papal teaching.

After the inaugural Mass of Francis's pontificate, *America* magazine chose him for their cover picture on April 20, 2013, and anticipated a major theme of his practice and teaching by showing him embracing a child with a disability. On September 30, 2013, even before *Evangelii Gaudium* (the Joy of the Gospel) appeared on November 26, 2013, *America* magazine enjoyed a scoop, conversations with Pope Francis that originated with three meetings the previous August: "A Big Heart Open to God: An Interview with Antonio Spadaro, SJ." The interview was shared with several other Jesuit journals. The editors of these journals prepared questions for Spadaro, the editor of *Civiltà Cattolica*, who conducted the interview with the pope.

When Pope Francis issued *Evangelii Gaudium* (the Joy of the Gospel) on November 26, 2013, *America* welcomed this papal exhortation on evangelization in the modern world by presenting four responses (January 6–13, 2014). A Magna Carta for the reform of the whole

Catholic Church (including the papacy), *Evangelii Gaudium* expanded one of Avery Dulles's images for the Church (community of disciples; see chap. 3 above) by expounding the Church as a community of missionary disciples (art. 24). With this exhortation, Francis established himself as the spiritual director to all Christians and, indeed, to the entire world. As the British journalist Austen Ivereigh put it during a March 2019 visit to Melbourne (Australia), "Francis is leading the Church on an Ignatian retreat."

Subsequent articles in *America* regularly recalled the teaching of *Evangelii Gaudium*. Bishop Robert W. McElroy picked up article 202 for his piece, "Market Assumptions: Pope Francis' Challenge to Income Inequality" (November 3, 2014). Gerard O'Connell appealed to articles 30, 31, and 33 in his "Call to Conversion" (December 8–15, 2014). Referencing the stress on dialogue found in *Evangelii Gaudium*, Drew Christiansen, SJ (now at Georgetown University), reviewed several works of "religious atheism" (February 2, 2015). A Latin American view of Pope Francis's theology (February 1, 2016) drew extensively on *Evangelii Gaudium* (217–37, 241).

America magazine did its best to spread the pope's model of the Church becoming a humble, listening Church of missionary disciples. It did the same for the encyclical letter on ecology and climate, *Laudato Si'* (Praise be [to you, my Lord]) of May 24, 2015. In the issue for May 26–June 1, 2015, it dedicated an article and a column to the encyclical.

America greeted *Amoris Laetitia* (the Joy of Love; March 19, 2016) by publishing "Portraits of Love: A Deeper Look at *Amoris Laetitia*," comments coming from several theologians (May 23–30, 2016). It followed this up by printing a conversation with Cardinal Christoph Schönborn on the teaching of *Amoris Laetitia* (August 15–22, 2016).

The lasting impact Pope Francis will have on the Society of Jesus in the United States and elsewhere, as well as on others through Jesuits, is obviously an unfinished story. It largely depends on what he can achieve in his chosen role of the world's "Spiritual Director."

We turn next to the contributions that American Jesuits made to the work of the Second Vatican Council and then to its interpretation and application.

CHAPTER 7

AMERICAN JESUITS AND THE SECOND VATICAN COUNCIL

FAR FROM BEING THE SOLE AGENTS, Jesuits did much, nevertheless, to mediate the events and teaching of the Second Vatican Council to Catholics and others in the United States and beyond. We can examine this record in three stages: during the Council itself (1962–65), the next twenty years (1965–85), and the decades that culminated in the fifty-year celebrations (2012–15) and their immediate aftermath. We begin with Vatican II's work in reforming and updating liturgy, theology, education, religious life, governance, canon law, and the rest, including relations with other Christians, non-Christians, and the world.[1]

This chapter will concentrate on what Jesuits in the United States did toward a positive reception of the Council. But, even if we do not investigate resistance to the teaching of Vatican II, we need to recognize that a few American and other Jesuits sided with those who rejected or at least played down the changes introduced by the Council. During the years that Vatican II met, not all Jesuits positively furthered the work of the bishops.[2]

DURING THE COUNCIL

Convoked by St. John XXIII (pope 1958–63), Vatican II met for one session under him and three under St. Paul VI (pope 1963–78).

John XXIII aimed at an *aggiornamento* (updating) of the Church's life and teaching. Instead of defining new dogmas, he wanted the Council to teach pastorally and encourage the cause of Christian and human unity.

The unprecedented number of non-European bishops present persuaded Karl Rahner to divide Christian history into three periods: (1) the Church at its origins in Jewish Christianity; (2) the Church of Hellenistic or Latin (European) culture, which lasted for many centuries; and (3) the Church of all nations, which started with Vatican II.

The Council was eventually attended by more than three thousand Catholic bishops. Appointments of new bishops continued and exceeded the deaths. This meant, for instance, that 150 of the bishops at the third session were participating for the first time in the Council. The numbers of non-Catholic observers and guests (Anglicans, Orthodox and Eastern Churches, and Protestants) grew more dramatically: from fifty-four (with eight guests) at the first session to 106 (with sixteen guests) at the fourth and final session. Their presence enhanced the value of Vatican II as a platform of dialogue and a point of reference for all Christians.[3]

During Vatican II, American Jesuits resident in Rome, especially those at the Gregorian University and the Biblical Institute, enjoyed frequent contacts with the bishops attending the Council, many of whom were alumni of their institutions or known to them in other ways. Some of those Jesuits offered evening "briefing" sessions to American and other bishops. Chapter 3 above recalled how effective Francis Sullivan, SJ, proved through a session at the North American College. He appealed to the New Testament in showing American bishops that all the baptized could be equipped with personal charisms in the service of the Church and the world. He drafted a text that, through one of those bishops, entered the relevant teaching of the Dogmatic Constitution on the Church (*Lumen Gentium* 12).

The first Vatican II document to be issued was *Sacrosanctum Concilium* (December 4, 1963), a constitution on the liturgy that endorsed reform and improved participation through (1) a return to earlier, simpler, and more intelligible forms; (2) a fuller use of the Bible; and (3) the possibility of using the vernacular or language of the place. The third session brought the Dogmatic Constitution on the Church, *Lumen Gentium*, also one of the Council's major achievements. It was approved on the same day (November 21, 1964) as the Decree on the

Catholic Churches of the Eastern Rite, *Orientalium Ecclesiarum*, and the Decree on Ecumenism, *Unitatis Redintegratio*, documents committing the Catholic Church to ecumenical initiatives that would bear fruit in official and unofficial dialogues. On October 28, 1965, the Council promulgated a decree on the training of priests, *Optatam Totius*, and a decree on the renewal of religious life, *Perfectae Caritatis*. The same day brought the much debated and highly significant *Nostra Aetate*, a declaration on the Church's relationship with Jews, Muslims, Hindus, Buddhists, and those of other faiths. On November 18, 1965, the Council fathers approved a document debated since the first session, *Dei Verbum*, a constitution on revelation that also dealt with faith, tradition, the Scriptures, the interpretation of the Gospels, and the role of the Scriptures in renewing the whole Church. On the last day of the Council, four documents were promulgated: a declaration on religious liberty, *Dignitatis Humanae*; a decree on the ministry and life of priests, *Presbyterorum Ordinis*; a decree on missionary activity, *Ad Gentes*; and the longest text of Vatican II, *Gaudium et Spes*, a pastoral constitution on the Church in the modern world.

Jesuits in the United States, aware that momentous history was being made at Vatican II, followed the proceedings and voting with vivid attention. Radio and television helped them to do so, as did such journals as *America*, *Civiltà Cattolica*, *Commonweal*, and the London *Tablet*—not to mention the *New York Times*, *Le Monde*, *La Croix*, and other newspapers. Reports from the American ecumenist Daniel J. O'Hanlon, SJ (1919–92), also kept alive interest in the progress of the Council. In 1961 he had coedited with the Protestant historian Heiko Oberman an important study, *Christianity Divided*. During the Council, O'Hanlon edited, with Yves Congar and Hans Küng, *Council Speeches of Vatican II* (1964). As a Council journalist, he was flanked by Francis Xavier Murphy (1914–2002), an American Redemptorist who, under the pseudonym of Xavier Rynne, wrote "Letters from Vatican City" for the *New Yorker*. These quickly appeared in four books, one for each session of the Council, which helped perpetuate a standard interpretation of Vatican II as "conservatives" versus "liberals, or "traditionalists" versus "progressives."[4]

A Jesuit at Boston College, Francis Sweeney, became involved in publicizing Vatican II. He used to invite overseas speakers to Boston College and made it possible for them to lecture also on other campuses. Sweeney knew the British actor, Alec Guinness, who valued a young Swiss theologian, Hans Küng (b. 1928), and recommended him to Sweeney. Küng had just published *The Council, Reform and Reunion*, was a professor of fundamental theology at the University of Tübingen, and had been appointed a *peritus* or official adviser at the Second Vatican Council. Thanks to Sweeney's invitation, in February 1963—and so between the first and second sessions of the Council—Küng arrived on an eight-week lecture tour of the United States.[5]

Catholic University of America had recently banned lectures by the Jesuits John Courtney Murray and Gustave Weigel; now they banned Küng from speaking about *The Council, Reform and Reunion* on their campus. A review by Joseph Clifford Fenton in the September 1962 issue of their house journal, *The American Ecclesiastical Review*, had vilified the book as "pure nonsense" and "a ridiculous hodge podge." The banning of Küng and the others produced, of course, the opposite effect.

Küng began his American tour by speaking to an audience of three thousand in the gymnasium of Boston College. He went on to lecture at Harvard, Yale, the University of Chicago (audience of five thousand), Gonzaga University (Spokane), the University of California in Los Angeles, and elsewhere. An audience of 8,500 heard him speak at the University of St. Louis, where he received the first honorary doctorate of his career. Back on the East Coast, he shared in an international theological dialogue, representing the Catholic side with Jean Daniélou, and engaged in dialogue with two eminent non-Catholics, Jaroslav Pelikan of Yale and Robert McAfee Brown (then at Stanford). Küng ended his series of lectures on "the Church & Freedom" at Georgetown University in Washington, DC. On the last day of his visit to the United States, he was welcomed at the White House by President John F. Kennedy.

During the four years when the Council met, one Canadian and two American Jesuits wrote articles in *Theological Studies* that concerned the making, respectively, of *Lumen Gentium*, *Dei Verbum*, and *Dignitatis Humanae*: David M. Stanley of Regis College, Toronto; Joseph A. Fitzmyer of Woodstock College; and John Courtney Murray of Woodstock College.

Thoroughly aware of the Council debates and preliminary voting (October 30, 1963) on episcopal "collegiality," Stanley published in June 1964 "The New Testament Basis for the Concept of Collegiality."[6] While not an official *peritus* at Vatican II, Stanley shared with the bishops and *periti* who read *Theological Studies* (and many other readers of the quarterly) the biblical warrant for the proposed teaching on collegiality. When promulgated on November 21, 1964, *Lumen Gentium* endorsed collegiality or the responsibility for the whole Church shared by the bishops in communion among themselves and with the head of the college of bishops, the pope (arts. 22–23).

Like Stanley,[7] *Lumen Gentium* (art. 22) noted that Christ gave the power of "binding and loosing" not only to Simon Peter but also to the college of the Twelve. But, unlike Stanley, the two articles dealing with collegiality did not appeal repeatedly to the scriptural witness. Those articles might have been strengthened by introducing the collegial continuity that Stanley drew between the missionary mandate and powers originally received by the Twelve, then by the postresurrection college of the Apostles (a wider group), and, finally, by the college of bishops today.

At the Council it was desirable to win acceptance for the two articles on collegiality from a minority of bishops and advisers initially opposed to this teaching. Hence the articles appealed to ecumenical councils, the fathers of the Church, canon law, and other traditional authorities (see notes 23–37 that accompany arts. 22–23). Vatican II's doctrinal commission added to the text of *Lumen Gentium* an appendix that presented the theological status of the teaching on collegiality. This was a last-minute attempt by the commission (and behind them Pope Paul VI) to allay the misgivings of a small minority who were more likely to be won over by traditional rather than biblical arguments.[8]

The Pontifical Biblical Commission's 1964 instruction on the historical truth of the Gospels, *Sancta Mater Ecclesia*,[9] drew strong support from Joseph Fitzmyer. In an article for *Theological Studies* he called the instruction "a positive document of no little importance." He summed up the value of *Sancta Mater Ecclesia*: "The document will go down in history as the first official statement which frankly admits the distinction of three stages" in the composition of the Gospels.[10] The following year the Constitution on Divine Revelation appealed to that instruction when presenting three stages in the formation of the Gospels: the eyewitness testimony to Jesus's ministry; the traditions about Jesus that were handed on orally or in writing; and the work of the evangelists in selecting, synthesizing, and explaining materials as they wrote their Gospels (*Dei Verbum* 19).

Here we should recall that, a year before the Council opened, Fitzmyer had discussed the historical truth of the Gospels in an article for *Theological Studies* that detailed attacks on the Biblical Institute that had come from the Lateran University: "A Recent Roman Controversy."[11] The following year (1962) copies of this article were distributed to the bishops assembled for the first session of Vatican II. At the Council the bishops received various handouts, like a replacement for the schema on "the sources of Revelation," drafted by Karl Rahner and Joseph Ratzinger and distributed to the bishops just before they began debating that schema in November 1962. But, as far as we know, the article of Fitzmyer was the only offprint from a theological quarterly handed out at the Council. It made *Theological Studies* effectively present even as Vatican II started and played its part in gathering support for the teaching on the Bible eventually found in the final text of *Dei Verbum*.

John Courtney Murray, the only American Jesuit to be a *peritus* at Vatican II, was deeply involved in drafting with Yves (later Cardinal) Congar, Johannes Feiner, and Pietro (later Cardinal) Pavan what was finally approved on the last day of the Council as *Dignitatis Humanae*. His extremely long article, published a year earlier in *Theological Studies*, "The Problem of Religious Freedom,"[12] served to prepare the way for the Council's declaration on religious liberty. He drew extensively on Pope John XXIII's 1963 encyclical, *Pacem in Terris*, which treated natural rights concerning life, education, and *religious freedom*—an encyclical that was repeatedly cited by *Dignitatis Humanae* as a major witness supporting the case for civil authority protecting the religious freedom and equality of all citizens. After the Council finished, Murray produced a follow-up article, expounding what he had helped to write, *Dignitatis Humanae*, and supplementing its meaning and message with relevant material from *Gaudium et Spes*: "The Issue of Church and State at Vatican Council II."[13]

THE RECEPTION FROM 1965 TO 1985

As soon as the Council ended on December 8, 1965, the task of studying, assimilating, and applying its sixteen documents began. How did Jesuits in the United States respond to the challenge of understanding and interpreting Vatican II?

In the reception of Vatican II promoted by American Jesuits and others, some of the Council's sixteen documents offered teaching that would be directly concerned with particular theological disciplines. *Sacrosanctum Concilium* became the Magna Carta for liturgical studies; the two constitutions on the Church, *Lumen Gentium* and *Gaudium et Spes*, impacted directly on ecclesiology; and *Unitatis Redintegratio* proved relevant for ecumenical studies and dialogue. *Nostra Aetate* provided a platform for interfaith learning and contacts. *Dei Verbum* fed into fundamental theology, scriptural studies, and biblically based prayer and life. *Perfectae Caritatis* called for a "return to the sources" of Christian life and prayer when reforming and updating the vocation of religious men and women.

In some areas what Vatican II served to promote concerned initiatives already taken by Jesuits in the United States. Liturgical developments built on the achievements of Gerald Ellard, who died at the start of the Council (chap. 6). Gustave Weigel, who had pioneered Jesuit ecumenical ecclesiology in the States, died in the second year of the Council but had already built bridges to other Christians (chap. 1). Joseph Fitzmyer had made his mark in scriptural studies before the Council (chap. 5) and did so during the Council as well. An American Jesuit "return to the sources" of Ignatian spirituality was already developing by the time Vatican II opened in 1962 (chap. 6).

In the reception of the Council by American Jesuits, Walter Abbott led the way. He had written for *America* an article on promoting ecumenism through the Bible. It attracted the attention of Cardinal Bea, who invited him to Rome, made him one of his staff, and allowed him to share firsthand in the proceedings of the Council.[14] Abbott organized a best-selling translation of the Council documents, introduced by brief but appropriate comments. The book was published as soon as Vatican II closed and sold over a million copies.

Theological Studies, the American Jesuit flagship among theological journals, was quick off the mark in running articles that commented on Vatican II's teaching. Some cited the Council's teaching when expounding specific topics. Thus William H. Dodd, SJ, drew repeatedly on Vatican II in "Toward a Theology of Priesthood."[15] The same was true of "Reflections on the Status of a Theology of the Layman" by William J. Kelly, SJ.[16] Raymond A. Adams, SJ, for his article "The Holy

Spirit and the Real Presence," used as a starting point the fact that the Spirit is hardly mentioned in the Constitution on the Sacred Liturgy and emphasized the importance of the *epiclesis* or eucharistic invocation of the Spirit.[17]

William H. Onclin, a canon lawyer from Louvain who had served as a *peritus* at the Council, in an article for *Theological Studies* titled "Church and Church Law" looked forward to what became the 1983 *Code of Canon Law* and the 1990 *Code of Canons of the Oriental Churches*: in "revised canon law...the principles established by the Council should find...both their fruitful expression and their integral application." Recalling Pope John XXIII's overriding motivation when he opened Vatican II, Onclin stated, "A pastoral concern should dominate in the fashioning of the Code." He ended with a central plea: "Last but not least, the new Code should above all and in all be conformed to the gospel message which Christ brought to the world. The prescriptions it contains must not deviate from it but, on the contrary, must be ever inspired by it."[18]

The Dogmatic Constitution on the Church, *Lumen Gentium*, showed up repeatedly in various articles. In the light of that document, George B. Wilson, SJ, treated "the gift of infallibility" in the final issue of *Theological Studies* for 1969. *Lumen Gentium* was also integral to the discussion in J. Robert Nelson's "Toward an Ecumenical Ecclesiology" (last issue in 1970).

Later articles often followed suit by using Vatican II teaching to illuminate and support their chosen theme. This would be the approach of David Hollenbach, SJ, in 1982[19] and Drew Christiansen, SJ, in 1984.[20] Twenty-five years later, authors appearing in *Theological Studies* continued to cite the Council when that was required by their subject. Joseph G. Mueller, SJ, attended to chapter 2 of *Dei Verbum* when discussing "Forgetting as Principle of Continuity in Tradition."[21] James G. McEvoy used *Gaudium et Spes* to launch his reflections on "Proclamation as Dialogue: Transition in the Church-World Relationship."[22]

Other articles concentrated on a specific theme in the Council's teaching or on a specific document. Paul Ramsey of Princeton University examined the relevant sections of *Gaudium et Spes* in "The Vatican Council on Modern War."[23] Gregory Baum, a Canadian *peritus* who had been marginally involved in drafting what became *Dei Verbum*, offered an account of "Vatican II's Constitution on Revelation: History and

Interpretation."[24] Manfred Hoffmann revealed his hopes in "Church and History in Vatican II's Constitution on the Church: A Protestant Perspective."[25] He looked for a coming Church that could hold together Catholicism and Protestantism in a unity where authority would make room for freedom, particularity, and progressive tradition. Leo J. O'Donovan, SJ, presented the influence of Pierre Teilhard de Chardin, SJ, on the Council's Pastoral Constitution on the Church in the Modern World: "Was Vatican II Evolutionary? A Note on Conciliar Language."[26] Years later Stephen Schloesser, SJ, would move beyond the question of language to state firmly, "Teilhard de Chardin's embrace of temporality was adopted at the council."[27]

Sometimes specific themes, such as the appeal in *Unitatis Redintegratio* to a certain "hierarchy" of revealed truths (art. 11), were taken up by more than one scholar. In *Theological Studies* for 1971, George H. Tavard published "*Hierarchia Veritatum*: A Preliminary Investigation." This article was followed in *Theological Studies* for 1987 by William Henn's "The Hierarchy of Truths Twenty Years Later."

MAJOR JESUIT INTERPRETERS

From the late 1960s, the interpretation and reception of the Second Vatican Council through articles in *Theological Studies* began featuring such major Jesuit contributors as John W. O'Malley, Avery Dulles, Jared Wicks, Karl Rahner, and (later) Francis A. Sullivan. In 1971, John W. O'Malley published "Reform, Historical Consciousness, and Vatican II's *Aggiornamento*"[28]—an early intimation of the outstanding work he was to publish on Vatican II and its predecessors in the sixteenth century (the Council of Trent) and the nineteenth century (Vatican I) (chap. 3 above). He continued to reveal his interest in Vatican II and rebutted those who wanted to play down the changes that brought a certain discontinuity with past teaching and practice: "Developments, Reforms, and the Two Great Reformations: Towards a Historical Assessment of Vatican II," and "Vatican II: Did Anything Happen?"[29] At one point he explored the implications and implementation of three documents of the Council: *Presbyterorum Ordinis* (on the "ministry and life of priests"), *Optatam Totius* (on the "training of priests"), and *Christus Dominus* (on the "pastoral office of bishops").

Far from satisfying him, these documents needed to be revised and enlarged.[30] Eventually O'Malley's interest in the Council flowered in the widely read book *What Happened at Vatican II* (2008), which was translated into at least six other languages.

The reflections that Avery Dulles offered on Vatican II blended into ecumenical concerns as the years moved on. In 1972, he published "The Church, the Churches, and the Catholic Church."[31] The following year, still very much in contact with *Lumen Gentium* and *Unitatis Redintegratio*, he produced another article: "Ministry and Intercommunion: Recent Ecumenical Statements and Debates."[32] An ecumenically minded ecclesiologist, Dulles would be appointed to the Lutheran–Roman Catholic Dialogue in the United States and serve on it for twenty years.

A doctorate at the University of Münster (for a dissertation on Martin Luther's instruction on Christian life) was enriched for Jared Wicks, a native of Columbus, Ohio, by contacts with professors of the Catholic and Evangelical theology faculties. They included Joseph Ratzinger, later Pope Benedict XVI, and Walter Kasper, later a cardinal and head of the Pontifical Council for Promoting Christian Unity. Wicks quickly followed up his doctoral studies with articles in *Theological Studies* on "Luther and the Person before God," "Abuses under Indictment at the Diet of Augsburg 1530," and "Justification and Faith in Luther's Theology."[33] Several books also showed Wicks practicing the ecumenical dialogue encouraged by Vatican II's *Unitatis Redintegratio*.[34] On commissions established for the Lutheran–Catholic dialogue, Wicks took part in discussions about justification (1986–93) and then about the apostolic character of the Church, which led to the study-document *The Apostolicity of the Church* (2007). He helped draft the landmark agreement *The Joint Declaration on the Doctrine of Justification*, signed by high officials of the Lutheran World Federation and the Catholic Church (October 31, 1999). All this work by Wicks exemplified splendidly the ecumenical activity recommended by Vatican II's Decree on Ecumenism, *Unitatis Redintegratio*.[35]

Arguably the major scoop on Vatican II for *Theological Studies* during the first twenty postconciliar years came in 1979. Weston School of Theology awarded Karl Rahner the honorary degree of Doctor of Humane Letters (April 8, 1979). The address he delivered on that occasion was published as "Towards the Fundamental Theological Interpretation of Vatican II."[36] In that address he divided Christian history into three periods, as we discussed earlier: the Church at her origins in Jewish Christianity; the Church of European culture, which lasted for many centuries; and the Church of all nations, which started with the Second Vatican Council itself.

From 1965 to 1985, Jesuits in the United States were doing much more than writing about Vatican II. It was being received and implemented at their high schools, colleges, universities, parishes, and theologates. T. Howland Sanks, SJ, published a vivid picture of what happened at the level of Jesuit theologates where Jesuits received their education for future ministry. He quoted, for example, the 1984 syllabus for the comprehensive examination toward a master of divinity at Alma College, which in 1969 had joined an ecumenical consortium (the Graduate Theological Union in Berkeley). Now in English rather than Latin, the syllabus referred only once explicitly to the documents of Vatican II (*Lumen Gentium* 8), but the terminology throughout the text matched the biblical and pastoral language of the Council's documents. Apropos of the changes in the curriculum, Sanks rightly cautioned against tracing all of them to Vatican II. The biblical, ecumenical, and liturgical movements—not to mention the return to the sources championed by the *Nouvelle Théologie*—which "preceded the Council and prepared for it were already being felt in the seminaries," not least the Jesuit seminaries. But "these stirrings" were given "further encouragement and impetus" by "the themes and emphases" of Vatican II.[37]

THE EXTRAORDINARY SYNOD OF 1985

In 1985 a fresh start came for Jesuits and others engaged in interpreting and receiving Vatican II. The 1985 Extraordinary Synod of Bishops met in Rome (November 24 to December 8) to celebrate the Second Vatican Council (which had ended twenty years earlier on December 8, 1965), to evaluate the Council's role in the postconciliar Church and to develop some principles for the further reception of its teaching.[38] Dulles helped to publicize the work of this synod.[39]

The Extraordinary Synod encouraged such major projects as the three volumes edited by René Latourelle, SJ, a former dean of theology at the Gregorian and still a professor there: *Vatican II: Assessment and Perspectives; Twenty-Five Years After (1962–1987)*.[40] Six American

Jesuits contributed chapters to these volumes: Avery Dulles, Francis A. Sullivan, James H. Swetnam, Robert F. Taft, Robert A. White (a communications expert), and Jared Wicks. Three of these (Sullivan, White, and Wicks) were professors at the Gregorian; Swetnam taught at the Biblicum; and Taft was a professor at the Oriental Institute in Rome. Latourelle himself had volunteered to be a translator at the synod so that he could follow proceedings in person. Latourelle and the professors at the Gregorian, Biblicum, and Orientale who wrote chapters for his three volumes were both American and otherwise and both Jesuit and otherwise. They fostered among their students, the vast majority of whom came from outside Italy, a knowledge and appreciation of Vatican II.

American and other Jesuit professors encouraged students to write on questions directly connected with the Council. At the Gregorian, Wicks supervised seven doctoral dissertations on Vatican II (defended from 1987 to 2004), three of which appeared in the prestigious *Tesi Gregoriana* series.

Americans and others who read the *Gregorianum*, the Gregorian University's official quarterly in theology and philosophy, were affected by the renewed interest in Vatican II that followed the Extraordinary Synod of 1985. Immediately after the Council ended in December 1965, the *Gregorianum* published fifteen articles dealing with the conciliar documents (1966–69). After that promising start, for nearly twenty years (1970–86), the quarterly published little by way of interpreting, receiving, and applying the Council, only two articles (in 1971 and 1973) on its teaching about Scripture as "the soul of theology," and a 1975 article on the meaning of "charism" for Vatican II. But when Jacques Dupuis, SJ, became editor in 1985,[41] the year of the Synod, the *Gregorianum* began once again to function as a quarterly concerned to interpret and receive the conciliar teaching. From 1986 to 2003, it published twenty articles on Vatican II.

The Synod helped to prompt another major project: Giuseppe Alberigo and Joseph A. Komonchak (eds.), *History of Vatican II*, in five volumes.[42] Three American Jesuits, one a theologian and the other two church historians, served on the editorial board of this Italian-American project: Avery Dulles, Gerald Fogarty, and John O'Malley.

Since the acts of Vatican II were now fully published (1970 to 1980), further research into Vatican II could begin to flower. The records of conciliar commissions and other primary sources, such as diaries (e.g., the diaries of Otto Semmelroth and Yves Congar) and letters from those who participated in the Council, also became available for scholarly investigation. The experience of liturgical reforms, ecumenical and interfaith dialogues and agreements, episcopal conferences and synods, and other developments also threw fresh light on such Vatican texts as *Sacrosanctum Concilium*, *Lumen Gentium*, *Unitatis Redintegratio*, *Nostra Aetate*, and *Dei Verbum*. Publications on the Council began to pick up again. In 1993, it took a fifty-page bibliography to record what had been written (since 1965) on *Dei Verbum*, the Dogmatic Constitution on Divine Revelation.[43]

RECEPTION OF VATICAN II: FROM 1985 TO 2012

Valuable articles on Vatican II continued to appear regularly in *Theological Studies*: for instance, in 2001 Ormond Rush on a key expression used by *Lumen Gentium* 12 and *Dei Verbum* 8 ("*Sensus Fidei*: Faith 'Making Sense' of Revelation"); in 2008 Thomas Hughson, SJ, on "Interpreting Vatican II: 'A New Pentecost'"); in 2010 Neil Ormerod on "Vatican II: Continuity or Discontinuity? Towards an Ontology of Meaning").[44]

Three important articles appeared in 2011. First, Francis A. Sullivan was encouraged by Vatican II's insistence on the truly universal saving will of God to argue in the March issue that infants who die unbaptized go to Christ and remain with him forever. In the same issue Stephen Bullivant explored, in the light of the Council's teaching, the question of salvation for those who are inculpably ignorant of the Gospel of Christ and his Church. In the September issue, Elizabeth T. Groppe revisited "Vatican II's Theology of the People of God after Forty-Five Years of Catholic-Jewish Dialogue."[45]

Clooney, Sullivan, and Wicks

In the period of reception that ran from 1986 to 2011, articles by Francis X. Clooney, SJ, Francis A. Sullivan, SJ, and Jared Wicks, SJ, in *Theological Studies* and other publications exemplified a desire to take further Vatican II's dialogue with other faiths and a desire to establish what the Council taught on ecclesiology and on the divine self-revelation.

(1) An earlier article by J. Peter Schineller, SJ, "Christ and the Church: A Spectrum of Views,"[46] had offered a fourfold classification of views current in the theology of religions ten years after the Council had ended: an ecclesiocentric universe, with an exclusive Christology; a Christocentric universe, with an inclusive, constitutive Christology; a theocentric universe, with a normative Christology; and a theocentric universe, with a non-normative Christology. This scheme was widely received and debated.

Jacques Dupuis, in his monumental *Toward a Christian Theology of Religious Pluralism*, dedicated several pages to Schineller's classification: "Though incomplete today, [it] retains some validity, and has the merit of putting in sharp relief a double paradigm shift as opinions changed from an ecclesiocentric worldview to a Christocentric one, and from a Christocentric to a theocentric." He added, "Despite the admitted merits of a fourfold grouping, many recent authors prefer a tripartite division of opinions. They distinguish three fundamental perspectives: ecclesiocentric, Christocentric, and theocentric, and, in parallel with these, three basic positions, respectively designated exclusivism, inclusivism, and pluralism."[47] Praising Schineller for having highlighted the paradigm shift, Dupuis himself preferred to describe his own position as "inclusive pluralism."

In developing his own "inclusive pluralism," Dupuis repeatedly made use of a study by the New England Jesuit Francis A. Sullivan, *Salvation Outside the Church? Tracing the History of the Catholic Response*.[48] As we noted in chapter 3, Sullivan not only contributed to the Festschrift honoring Dupuis on the occasion of his eightieth birthday, but he did so by writing about Clement of Alexandria's continuing relevance for those who discuss the saving function of non-Christian religions. In a 2012 book edited by James L. Heft and John O'Malley, *Vatican II: Trajectories and Hermeneutics*, Sullivan contributed a chapter about Vatican II and the postconciliar magisterium on the salvation of those who followed "other" religions.[49]

Through articles in *Theological Studies*, Sullivan had much to say when interpreting Vatican II's teaching on the magisterium and on the Church of Christ continuing to exist (*subsistit in*) fully (but not exclusively) in the Catholic Church. In chapter 3, we recalled his repeated contributions on these two questions.

(2) With an article entitled "Vedanta, Theology, and Modernity: A Case Study in Theology's New Conversation with the World's Religions,"[50] Francis Xavier Clooney, a New York Jesuit who taught at Boston College before moving to a chair at Harvard, creatively developed the study of other faiths and the dialogue with them that Vatican II's *Nostra Aetate* invited. A few years later Clooney used a benchmark term that would summarize his coming contributions: "Comparative Theology: A Review of Recent Books."[51] Comparative theology would sum up the program of learning interreligiously developed in his *Comparative Theology: Deep Learning across Religious Borders* (2010) and *His Hiding Place Is Darkness: A Hindu-Christian Theopoetics of Divine Absence* (2014).[52]

(3) After years of research into Luther and Reformation theology, Wicks directed his attention toward the Council itself and the pope who convoked it: "Tridentine Motivations of Pope John XXIII before and during Vatican II."[53] He investigated as well the input of the *periti*, or official consultors, toward the drafting of the Constitution on Divine Revelation, *Dei Verbum*.[54] He supplied rich documentation about their work, not least the five articles he published on Pieter Smulders, SJ, and the making of *Dei Verbum* (in the *Gregorianum* for 2001 [two articles], 2002, 2004, and 2005). A long chapter in his *Doing Theology* (Paulist Press, 2009) examined the ways and means by which theologians contributed to the work and success of the Council.[55] He wrote for the *Gregorianum* in 2003 an extended review of the French original of Congar's *My Journal of the Council*, which had just appeared for the first time. In the *Gregorianum* for 2008 he published and commented on six texts prepared by Joseph Ratzinger as a *peritus* before and during Vatican II. For a Festschrift in honor of Robert Imbelli, he has reproduced with commentary a seventh text by Ratzinger (October 15, 1962).[56] This text led to collaboration with Karl Rahner in producing, as an alternative to the official schema on "the Sources of Revelation," a replacement text distributed to the bishops in November 1962 just before they began discussing that schema.

In 2006, Wicks began a series called "Light on Vatican II" for the *Catholic Historical Review*. In 2019 he published, for example, a study of the genesis and itinerary of what eventually became a chapter in *Lumen Gentium* on the Blessed Virgin Mary (arts. 52–69). In all, he wrote eight articles for this series.

At the commencement ceremony in May 2007, John Carroll

University in Cleveland, Ohio, awarded honorary doctorates to Wicks, O'Malley, and O'Collins. It was a way of recognizing their continuing work in the cause of interpreting and promoting the teaching and invitations of Vatican II. O'Collins had already published *Living Vatican II: The 21st Council for the 21st Century* (2006; awarded first prize in its section by the Catholic Press Association), and would publish *The Second Vatican Council on Other Religions* (2013), *The Spirituality of the Second Vatican Council* (2014), *The Second Vatican Council: Message and Meaning* (2014), and the entry "Vatican II, Jesuits and" for the *Cambridge Encyclopedia of Jesuits* (2017).

RECEPTION OF VATICAN II: FROM 2012 TO 2018

American Jesuits welcomed in various ways the fifty-year celebration of the Second Vatican Council (2012–15). Loyola University Chicago, for instance, staged a conference on "The Spirit of Vatican II: Then and Now" (September 20, 2012). The School of Theology and Ministry at Boston College held a highly successful symposium on "The Legacy of Vatican II" (September 26, 2013).

Theological Studies excelled in its coverage. In 2012 it presented six articles on the Council. They included two articles that took the large view: Ormond Rush's "Toward a Comprehensive Interpretation of the Council and Its Documents" and an article by John O'Malley on changes introduced by Vatican II ("The Hermeneutic of Reform: A Historical Analysis").

In 2013 the eleven articles on Vatican II that appeared in *Theological Studies* included articles examining a specific document or a specific section in one of the Council's documents: for instance, Mary C. Boys, "What *Nostra Aetate* Inaugurated: A Conversion to the 'Providential Mystery of Otherness'"; and Jared Wicks, "Spiritual Reading Urged *Vehementer* (*Dei Verbum*, 25): Background and Development." That year *Theological Studies* also published more general articles on the Council: for instance, Anne Hunt, "The Trinitarian Depths of Vatican II"; James F. Keenan, SJ, "Vatican II and Theological Ethics"; Peter C. Phan, "Reception of and Prospects for Vatican II in Asia"; and Gilles Routhier, "Vatican II: Relevance and Future."

Theological Studies featured three more articles on the Council in 2014. They were led in the March issue by Ladislas Orsy's "The Divine Dignity of Human Persons in *Dignitatis Humanae*." Fifty years after the Second Vatican Council, this Jesuit canon lawyer tackled the still highly relevant question: How ought the Church respect the consciences of free and intelligent human beings, created in the divine image and replicas of divine nature?

In 2015 *Theological Studies* published five articles that involved Vatican II's teaching and decision-making. For those concerned with ecclesiology or the theology of the Church, the most interesting piece came in the March issue: Dennis M. Doyle on "Otto Semmelroth and the Advance of the Church as Sacrament at Vatican II." Today Semmelroth belongs among the nearly forgotten *periti*. But at the Council he played a major part toward introducing the notion of the Church as sacrament and overcoming opposition coming from Cardinal Ernesto Ruffini and his friend, Joseph Clifford Fenton.

To crown this splendid achievement in publication, in late 2015 David G. Schultenover, SJ, the outgoing editor of *Theological Studies*, brought together in *50 Years On: Probing the Riches of Vatican II* sixteen articles on Vatican II already published by *Theological Studies* over the four years of celebration. For this work in collaboration on the Council, Stephen Schloesser wrote a long introduction. In *Theological Studies* for 2006, he had already published an elegant article on Vatican II, "Against Forgetting: Memory, History, Vatican II."

Theological Studies could hardly have done more to receive, interpret, and apply the teaching of Vatican II on the occasion of the Council's fiftieth anniversary. Under its new editor in chief, Paul G. Crowley, SJ (b. 1945), the quarterly has continued to keep the Council before its readers. He had already displayed his commitment to a life-giving retrieval of Vatican II by editing *From Vatican II to Pope Francis: Charting a Catholic Future* (Orbis Books, 2014).

In *Theological Studies* for March 2016, Grant Kaplan documented influences on the renewal of ecclesiastical studies embodied in Vatican II's decree on priestly formation, *Optatam Totius*. In December that year, Gerald O'Collins introduced his discussion of Pope Francis's exhortation *Amoris Laetitia* (the Joy of Love) by recalling the teaching of the Second Vatican Council on marriage and the family.

The March 2017 issue of *Theological Studies* featured articles on two Vatican II documents, *Dei Verbum* and *Nostra Aetate*, as well as

Declan Marmion's "Karl Rahner, Vatican II, and the Shape of the Church." In the June issue, Ormond Rush argued that Vatican II's teaching on the *sensus fidelium* supported Pope Francis's vision of a synodal Church. In the very next issue, September 2017, he proposed that Catholic discernment of the *sensus fidelium*, as presupposed by *Lumen Gentium* 12, should also include the *sensus fidei* of other Christians. Another article in this same issue explored the shift represented by *Gaudium et Spes* from a theology of history to a Christian anthropology. The December number of *Theological Studies* featured an article that used Vatican II teaching to develop a vision of deacons as representing Christ the servant. Altogether seven articles in *Theological Studies* for 2017 revealed the ongoing significance of the Council for those reflecting on anthropological, ecclesial, ecumenical, interfaith, ministerial, and other questions.

Theological Studies opened 2018 by running one article (in its March issue) on Vatican II debates over episcopal collegiality and another article on Orthodox observers at the Council. The September issue presented Rafael Luciani on the Second General Conference of the Latin American Episcopate (Medellín, 1968). He showed how it represented the reception of *Gaudium et Spes* within the "People of God" ecclesiology of *Lumen Gentium*. Medellín remains the only example of a continental reception of Vatican II carried out in a collegial and synodal manner. In the final issue for 2018, Catherine E. Clifford examined a major reason for valuing highly O'Malley's work on the Council: "Style Is Substance: Origins of John W. O'Malley's Contribution to the Interpretation of Vatican II." With Massimo Faggioli, Clifford is the coeditor of the forthcoming *Oxford Handbook of Vatican II*.

In the London *Tablet* for Christmas 2002, Cardinal Franz König wrote, "The crucial process of reception, that all-important part of any church council…can take several generations. It continues today." American Jesuits have done much for that "crucial process," and they continue to contribute to the "all-important" reception of Vatican II.

This chapter has dwelt largely on what Jesuits published in books and articles that interpreted and applied the teaching of Vatican II. This, of course, is only one important part of the story. A comprehensive account of American Jesuits receiving the Council would involve examining what happened in their communities, parishes, high schools, colleges, universities, theologates, and other scenes of their life and ministry. That would require at least one large volume.

CONCLUSIONS

How have those who were served and influenced by Jesuit theologians and philosophers in the United States evaluated what they received? What have these "customers" and others judged the Jesuit contribution to have been, whether it came through colleges, universities, high schools, seminaries, parishes, professional or popular associations and publications, or in other ways?

PUBLIC RECOGNITION

In earlier chapters we occasionally offered a sample of such reactions. Chapter 1, for example, recalled the very public way in which Pope Paul VI expressed esteem for the role that John Courtney Murray played in bringing about Vatican II's Declaration on Religious Liberty. He invited Murray to concelebrate Mass with him. The same chapter ended by quoting the Princeton theologian George Hunsinger's appreciation of what he received from Jesuit teachers when doing his basic theological studies within the Boston Theological Institute and just after the Council. Chapters 1 and 5 detailed the high regard in which Joseph Fitzmyer was held by his biblical colleagues, Catholic and otherwise. Chapter 5 also revealed the standing of another Jesuit scriptural scholar, George MacRae. At the time of his tragically unexpected death, he had just begun an appointment as acting dean of Harvard Divinity School and was widely tipped to become the permanent dean.

Chapter 2 recalled the public recognition of some Jesuit philosophers. Walter Ong not only lectured around the world but also was honored by being elected president of the powerful Modern Language Association (1978). When summarizing in the same chapter the achievements of Norris Clarke, we noted how in 1980 he received the Aquinas Medal from the American Catholic Philosophical Association. Some of the other Jesuit recipients of this medal were Bernard Lonergan (1970), Frederick Copleston (1977), and Quentin Lauer (1985).

Walter Burghardt received twenty-three honorary doctorates from universities across the United States. In 1985 the Catholic University of America established the Johannes Quasten Award as the only academic award given each year by the university's School of Theology and Religious Studies. So far, seven Jesuits have received the Quasten Award: Brian Daley, John Donahue, Joseph Fitzmyer, Gerald O'Collins, John O'Malley, Robert Taft, and Jared Wicks.

Another book could explore in full detail what Jesuit theologians and philosophers contributed to such associations as the American Academy of Religion, the Catholic Biblical Association, the Catholic Theological Society of America, the College Theology Society, and the Society of Biblical Literature. Over many decades Jesuits have been involved in these and other associations. Detailed research could reveal their input and influence.

NEGATIVE INFLUENCES

We aimed in this book to present the positive and life-giving input Jesuits have made to philosophy and theology in the United States. Here and there we mentioned the negative influence some Jesuits exercised: for instance, Anthony Maas, who rigidly resisted developments in biblical scholarship (chap. 5), and those, many years later, who conspired to remove the excellent 1991 translation of the psalter (chap. 5).

We could have added on the "negative" side other names like that of Leonard Feeney (1897–1978).[1] He died reconciled to the Catholic Church but only after being dismissed from the Society of Jesus and excommunicated for propagating in the strictest sense that salvation was impossible for those "outside the Church." He also lashed out at Harvard (a "pest hole") and accused the archbishop of Boston, Richard (later Cardinal) Cushing, of watering down Catholic faith by dining and speaking at Harvard.

A Jesuit astronomer, remembered for his work on variable stars, Daniel J. K. O'Connell (1896–1982), had studied at Harvard College Observatory and became director of the Vatican Observatory (1952–70). He told O'Collins about an incident when he was staying in the same community as Feeney. Angrily denouncing Harvard, Feeney tried to physically stop O'Connell from heading off one morning to the Harvard Observatory. In the fall of 1968, O'Collins visited Cardinal Cushing who recalled episodes that led up to Feeney being excommunicated by the Holy See (February 13, 1953): "I invited him to visit me. When I stepped into the room, Feeney stood up, shook a finger at me, and declared in a loud voice: 'In the name of Mary Immaculate, I excommunicate you.'" "Well," the cardinal added with a smile, "he really caught me with my pants down."

Maas, Feeney, and others are regularly assigned to the "conservative" extreme. We could also speak of a few Jesuit theologians who seem to have moved to an opposite, "liberal" extreme. They appeared to prize alleged relevance over life-giving orthodoxy. But this book has concentrated on Jesuit philosophers and theologians of the broad, progressive "middle." They have known how to keep faith with the foundational revelation in Jesus Christ and with the Church's living tradition, while practicing an open hope that is not a mere repetition of what has gone before. Their teaching and writing have exercised and continue to exercise an illuminating and life-giving impact.

ASSESSMENTS

From recent times we might retrieve what American Jesuits involved in parishes, retreat and spirituality centers, high schools, colleges, universities, theologates, think tanks (like the Woodstock Center), and ministries in Africa, Asia, and elsewhere wanted their contribution in theology (and philosophy) to become. Their mission statements reveal their hopes and commitments.

It could well be even more illuminating, however, to gather assessments from those who studied theology and/or philosophy at one of the institutions just mentioned. One could also collect views from those theologians and philosophers who never studied with Jesuits but who regularly use material published by Jesuits or belong to the same professional organizations (e.g., the Catholic Biblical Association). We would need to hear not only from "fans" of Jesuits like George Hunsinger but also from less than fully satisfied "customers."

Such a survey would cover a variety of institutions and a variety of ages (e.g., up to twenty-five; twenty-five to fifty; fifty and above). It would also go beyond a handful of individuals chosen more or less at random and offer large samples.

Our work never attempted such a survey. But it could be a valuable project. We leave this project to others, recognizing how it would run to book length and complement what we have offered in our volume.

At the end of chapter 5, we noted that nowadays fewer American Jesuits show up among the ranks of leading biblical scholars—something that is true in other fields of theology as well. This change was inevitable, given the fact that the numbers of Jesuits in the United States fell by more than half between 1982 and 2010. The place of the Jesuits in departments of philosophy, religious studies, and theology has been partly taken by well-prepared laypersons, who have often studied with Jesuit professors and are shaped by Ignatian spirituality.

The same change has been taking place in leadership roles. By May 2019, sixteen out of the twenty-eight Jesuit colleges and universities in the Association of Jesuit Colleges and Universities (AJCU) were led by lay presidents, three of whom were women. The consolidation of the Jesuit-run University of Detroit and the Mercy College of Detroit led to Sr. Maureen A. Fay, a member of the Adrian Dominican community, becoming the first president of University of Detroit Mercy (1990–2004). In 2001, John J. DeGoia became president of Georgetown University, the first layperson appointed to this role. The AJCU institutions continue to seek ways and means to live out more fully their original Jesuit mission.

Not written in a spirit of self-congratulation that would proudly glorify the past and sing the praises of our Jesuit predecessors, this book has retrieved achievements from a story that has run for well over two hundred years. It has aimed to inspire Jesuits and others into becoming better theologians and philosophers, who will bring more and more people to be closer and more effective followers of Jesus Christ. We remain convinced that this mission can find a source of enlightenment and encouragement in the history of what Jesuits have already done to further the cause of theology and philosophy in the United States.

NOTES

CHAPTER 1

1. See Anthony Kuzniewski, SJ, "Maryland Mission," *CEJ*, 507–9.

2. See Thomas Murphy, SJ, "United States of America," *CEJ*, 797–802; Raymond A. Schroth, SJ, *The American Jesuits: A History* (New York: New York University Press, 2007).

3. On Carroll, see R. Emmett Curran, SJ, et al., *American Jesuit Spirituality: The Maryland Tradition, 1634–1900* (Baltimore: Corporation of Roman Catholic Clergymen, 1976); Peter Guilday, *The Life and Times of John Carroll* (Westminster, MD: Newman Press, 1954; orig. 1922); Thomas O. Hanley, ed., *The John Carroll Papers*, 3 vols. (Notre Dame, IN: University of Notre Dame Press, 1976; hereafter *JCP*); Annabelle M. Melville, *John Carroll of Baltimore* (New York: Charles Scribner's Sons, 1955); Thomas Murphy, SJ, "Carroll, John, SJ," *CEJ*, 139–41; Thomas W. Spalding, *The Premier See: A History of the Archdiocese of Baltimore, 1789–1989* (Baltimore: Johns Hopkins University Press, 1989).

4. Apropos of studies at the Jesuit house in Liège, Carroll wrote in a letter of February 12, 1803, to his long-standing friend Charles Plowden: "It seemed to me that at Liège, far from encouraging young men to extend the circle of their knowledge, the heads of the College esteemed no merit but that of the study of their dictates. The little of Greek which had been learned at St. Omer or Bruges was suffered to perish; the Hebrew lesson was a mere mockery, even the cultivation of Latin elegance was thrown aside; and as to our native language, there was scarcely a book of it in the library worthy of being studied. No

modern author of any science or of any language was introduced into it. Thus genius & talent were cramped, & a habit of inapplication was acquired, which few escaped" (*JCP*, vol. 2, 409).

5. *JCP*, vol. 1, 6.

6. Carroll had been released by his superiors to accompany a young English nobleman, Charles Philip, sixteenth Lord Stourton (1752–1816), on this "grand tour." A direct descendant (great-great-great-great-grandson), Edward Stourton of the BBC, interviewed one of us (O'Collins) a number of times—in particular, for Radio 4's coverage of St. John Paul II's funeral (April 6, 2005).

7. Charles E. O'Neill, "John Carroll, the 'Catholic Enlightenment' and Rome," in *American Catholic Preaching and Piety in the Time of John Carroll*, ed. Raymond J. Kupke (Lanham, MD: University Press of America, 1991), 1–26, at 15. Carroll never referred to Pope Clement XIV as such; he called him "Ganganelli."

8. *JCP*, vol. 1, 27, 29.

9. *JCP*, vol. 1, 32.

10. *JCP*, vol. 1, 46–50.

11. *JCP*, vol. 1, 252.

12. O'Neill, "John Carroll," 12.

13. In the longest piece of writing left by Carroll, *An Address to the Roman Catholics of the United States of America by a Catholic Clergyman* (from late 1884; *JCP*, vol. 1, 82–144), he was clear on the need to follow one's conscience. He put this rhetorical question: "After mature inquiries, if I am convinced that the religion of England is the only true one, am I not obliged to become a protestant?" (87). Carroll wanted Georgetown University to respect freedom of conscience and be open to students of different faiths; see G. Roland Murphy, SJ, "Georgetown's Shield: *Utraque Unum*," in *Splendor and Wonder: Jesuit Character, Georgetown Spirit, and Liberal Education*, ed. William J. O'Brien (Washington, DC: Georgetown University Press, 1988), 23–38, at 28–32.

14. *JCP*, vol. 1, 51.

15. *JCP*, vol. 1, 80–81.

16. New York: Sheed & Ward, 1960.

17. R. Emmett Curran, SJ, "Georgetown's Self-Image at Its Centenary," in *Georgetown at Two Hundred: Faculty Reflections on the University's Future*, ed. William C. McFadden, SJ (Washington, DC: Georgetown University Press, 1990), 1–17, at 5; Anthony Kuzniewski,

SJ, "Georgetown University," *CEJ*, 326–28. For the early history of Georgetown, see Curran, *The Bicentennial History of Georgetown University: From Academy to University 1789–1889*, vol. 1 (Washington, DC: Georgetown University Press, 1993).

18. *JCP*, vol. 1, 240–47, at 241.

19. *JCP*, vol. 1, 243; see Curran, *The Bicentennial History*, vol. 1, 42–44; Dorothy M. Brown, "Learning, Faith, Freedom, and Building a Curriculum: Two Hundred Years and Counting," in *Georgetown at Two Hundred*, 79–108, at 80–83.

20. McFadden, "Catechism at 4 for all the Schools: Religious Instruction at Georgetown," in McFadden, *Georgetown at Two Hundred*, 143–68.

21. See J. C. Murray, "Towards a Theology for the Layman: The Problem of Its Finality," *TS* 5 (1944): 43–75; "Toward a Theology for the Layman: The Pedagogical Problem," *TS* 5 (1944): 340–76.

22. McFadden, "Catechism at 4," 150–53.

23. The youngest of these twenty-eight was Wheeling College, founded in 1954, becoming Wheeling Jesuit University in 1996. Its Jesuit affiliation ceased in 2019. The *CEJ* includes entries on Boston College, Georgetown University, Saint Louis University, and the University of San Francisco. See also Cinthia Gannett, "Universities, 1773–Present," *CEJ*, 806–8. Mary Ann Hinsdale, "Scandals," *CEJ*, 715, includes an account of the scandalous affair of 1838, when 272 slaves owned by Maryland Jesuits were sold by a former president of Georgetown and part of the profits passed on to the university.

24. On the growth of Jesuit colleges and universities, see Schroth, *The American Jesuits*, 61–63.

25. O'Neill, "John Carroll," 17.

26. *JCP*, vol. 1, 105–6.

27. *JCP*, vol. 2, 202–3.

28. London: Burns & Oates, 1953.

29. Palmer, *Mary*, 79.

30. Schroth, *The American Jesuits*, 51–56.

31. See P. J. Dooley, SJ, "Woodstock and Its Makers," *Woodstock Letters* 56 (1927): 3–112.

32. Schroth, *The American Jesuits*, 88.

33. On the original staff, see Dooley, "Woodstock," 26–38.

34. Dooley, "Woodstock," 29; on Mazzella, see Schroth, *The American Jesuits*, 95–96.

35. Dooley, "Woodstock," 31. Francisco Suárez, SJ (1548–1617), taught at Salamanca (1592–96).

36. McFadden, "Religious Instruction at Georgetown," in *Georgetown at Two Hundred*, 143–68, at 167n47.

37. (New York: P. F. Collier, 1891), 182.

38. "An Explanation in Reply to Some Recent Strictures," *Woodstock Letters* 26 (1897): 147.

39. R. Emmett Curran, SJ, ed., *American Jesuit Spirituality: The Maryland Tradition, 1634–1900* (Mahwah, NJ: Paulist Press, 1988), 151–61.

40. *JCP*, vol. 2, 96.

41. Curran, *American Jesuit Spirituality*, 28, 35–37.

42. See Jared Wicks, SJ, "Theology, Manualist," in *Dictionary of Fundamental Theology*, ed. René Latourelle, SJ, and Rino Fisichella (New York: Crossroad, 1996), 1102–5; G. O'Collins, *The Second Vatican Council: Message and Meaning* (Collegeville, MN: Liturgical Press, 2014), 4–8.

43. Karl Rahner, SJ, "The Prospects for Dogmatic Theology," in *Theological Investigations*, vol. 1 (London: Darton, Longman & Todd, 1961), 1–18, at 4.

44. See Oliver P. Rafferty, SJ, "The Thomistic Revival and the Relationships between the Jesuits and the Papacy 1878–1914," *TS* 75 (2014): 746–73; and Gerald A. McCool, SJ, *Nineteenth-Century Scholasticism: The Search for a Unitary Method* (New York: Fordham University Press, 1996); and McCool, *The Neothomists* (Milwaukee: Marquette University Press, 1994).

45. See Oliver P. Rafferty, SJ, "George Tyrrell," *CEJ*, 793–94.

46. See Gilbert Joseph Garraghan, SJ, *The Jesuits of the Middle United States*, 3 vols. (Chicago: Loyola University Press, 1963–84); and Gerald McKevitt, SJ, *Brokers of Culture: Italian Jesuits in the American West* (Stanford, CA: Stanford University Press, 2007).

47. See Thomas Murphy, SJ, "Native Americans," *CEJ*, 549–51.

48. See Justin Poché, "De Smet, Peter John, SJ," *CEJ*, 226–28.

49. See Oliver P. Rafferty, SJ, ed., *George Tyrrell and Catholic Modernism* (Dublin: Four Courts Press, 2010); David G. Schultenhover, SJ, *George Tyrrell in Search of Catholicism* (Shepherdstown, UK: Patmos Press, 1982); Joseph P. Whelan, SJ, *The Spirituality of Friedrich von Hügel* (London: Collins, 1971).

50. On Lord, see Keith Maczkiewicz, SJ, "Lord, Daniel, SJ," *CEJ*,

476–77; and Schroth, *The American Jesuits*, 124–26. On LaFarge, see Peter McDonough, *Men Astutely Trained: A History of the Jesuits in the American Century* (New York: The Free Press, 1992), 118–35; J. Poché, "LaFarge, John, SJ," *CEJ*, 451–53; and Schroth, *The American Jesuits*, 117–24.

51. McDonough, *Men Astutely Trained*, 134–35. See Georges Passelecq and Bermond Suchecky, *The Hidden Encyclical of Pius XI* (New York: Harcourt Brace, 1997).

52. See Susan K. Wood, "Nouvelle Théologie," *CEJ*, 561–63; Wood, "Sources Chrétiennes," *CEJ*, 749–50.

53. See his memoir, *Late Have I Loved You: A Theologian Reflects on His Church* (Maryknoll, NY: Orbis Books, 2004); and Patrick J. Howell, SJ, "Burghardt, Walter J., SJ," *CEJ*, 125–26.

54. See Fitzmyer's devastating critique in *TS* 67 (2006): 410–11; Allegro took fifteen years to publish twenty-nine fragments and made a hash of it.

55. Westminster, MD: Newman Press, 1957.

56. New York: Doubleday, 1960; see Mary Ann Hinsdale, "Weigel, Gustave, SJ," *CEJ*, 838–39.

57. See Mary Ann Hinsdale, "Weigel, Gustave, SJ," *CEJ*, 838–40.

58. See William A. Clark, SJ, "Murray, John Courtney, SJ," *CEJ*, 535–36; McDonough, *Men Astutely Trained*, 214–41.

59. One of the students at Harvard Divinity School "felt" that his "theological education was saved by the Jesuits" (George O. Hunsinger, *The Beatitudes* [Mahwah, NJ: Paulist Press, 2015], xii). With a PhD from Yale, Hunsinger is a professor of systematic theology at Princeton Theological Seminary; he is a world expert on the thought of Karl Barth. In the spring of 2019, he was a visiting professor at the Gregorian University.

CHAPTER 2

1. This neo-Scholastic philosophy often looked unchanging and disengaged from contemporary challenges. Nicholas Russo, SJ (1845–1902), taught for only one year at Georgetown, but his Latin text on logic and metaphysics, *Summa Philosophica juxta Scholasticorum Principia* (1885), continued to be an assigned text until after the First World War.

2. See John B. Brough, "Philosophy at Georgetown University," in *Georgetown at Two Hundred: Faculty Reflections on the University's Future*, ed. William C. McFadden, SJ (Washington, DC: Georgetown University Press, 1990), 109–41; Peter Schineller, SJ, "Course of Studies," *CEJ*, 206–8; and Joseph A. Tetlow, SJ, "In *Oratione Directa*: Philosophy in the Jesuit Liberal Arts Curriculum in the United States," in *Jesuit Higher Education: Essays on an American Tradition of Excellence*, ed. Rolando E. Bonachea (Pittsburgh: Duquesne University Press, 1989), 105–23.

3. See David R. Foster and Joseph W. Koterski, SJ, eds., *The Two Wings of Catholic Thought: Essays on* Fides et Ratio (Washington, DC: Catholic University of America Press, 2003); and Thomas G. Guarino, "*Fides et Ratio*: Theology and Contemporary Pluralism," *TS* 63 (2002): 675–700.

4. On "being philosophical," see G. O'Collins, *Rethinking Fundamental Theology: Toward a New Fundamental Theology* (Oxford: Oxford University Press, 2011), 334–36.

5. See James Bernauer, "Philosophy," *CEJ*, 611–12. When expounding "the books to be lectured on," the Jesuit *Constitutions* state that "in logic, natural and moral philosophy and metaphysics, the doctrine of Aristotle should be followed" (iv.14). See Bernard Knorn, SJ, "Theological Renewal after the Council of Trent? The Case of the Jesuit Commentaries on the *Summa Theologiae*," *TS* 79 (2018): 107–27.

6. See John Gavin, "Suárez," *CEJ*, 763–65.

7. *CEJ*, 764. In "Recent Works in Jesuit Philosophy: Vicissitudes of Rhetorical Accommodation," *Journal of Jesuit Studies* 1 (2014): 105–26, Stephen Schloesser discusses eight books, five of which treat the work of Suárez.

8. Schloesser, "Recent Works in Jesuit Philosophy," 111–12.

9. A famous neo-Thomist, Joseph Kleutgen, SJ, was a major contributor to *Aeterni Patris*, as he had been to the two documents of the First Vatican Council (1869–70), notably *Dei Filius* on which he worked with Johann Baptist Franzelin, SJ. Kleutgen's personal and priestly life proved scandalous; see Mary Ann Hinsdale, "Scandals," *CEJ*, 715–16.

10. Bernauer, "Philosophy," *CEJ*, 611.

11. Oliver P. Rafferty, SJ, "The Thomistic Revival and the Relationship between the Jesuits and the Papacy, 1878–1914," *TS* 75 (2014): 746–77, at 752–53.

12. Rafferty, "The Thomistic Revival," 771–72.

13. See Cathal Doherty, SJ, "The Symbiosis of Philosophy and Theology in Blondel's Supernatural Hypothesis," *TS* 79 (2018): 274–93; Oliva Blanchette, *Maurice Blondel: A Philosophical Life* (Grand Rapids, MI: Eerdmans, 2010). Born in 1929, Blanchette, dean of the School of Philosophy at Boston College (1968–73), was a Jesuit for a number of years before leaving and marrying.

14. *The American Jesuits: A History* (New York: New York University Press, 2007), 205–6.

15. Jacques Monet, SJ, and Frederick Crowe, SJ, "Bernard J. Lonergan, SJ," *CEJ*, 475–76.

16. See John W. Padberg, SJ, "Saint Louis University," *CEJ*, 706–7.

17. See James Bernauer, SJ, "Ong, Walter J., SJ," *CEJ*, 575–76.

18. David C. Paternostro, SJ, "Getting Personal: The Philosophy of Norris Clarke, SJ," *America*, May 11, 2015, 26–28.

19. We owe the two stories about Clarke to a personal communication from Paul Rourke, SJ.

20. (New York: Macmillan, 1996), 233–40; see also his short but brilliant article, "Heidegger and Theology," *TS* 26 (1965): 86–100.

21. See Henry Shea, SJ, "Copleston, Frederick, SJ," *CEJ*, 203–4.

22. F. Copleston, SJ, *A History of Philosophy*, vol. 9 (London: Search Press, 1975), 268n1.

23. J. Michelle Molina, "Molina, Luis de, SJ," *CEJ*, 526–27.

24. See Kenneth J. Perszyk, ed., *Molinism: The Contemporary Debate* (Oxford: Oxford University Press, 2011).

CHAPTER 3

1. See Charles Keenan, "Bellarmine, Robert, SJ, St.," *CEJ*, 91–93.

2. See Patrick W. Carey, *Avery Cardinal Dulles, SJ: A Model Theologian* (Mahwah, NJ: Paulist Press, 2010); Carey, "Dulles, Avery, Cardinal, SJ," *CEJ*, 244–49; G. O'Collins, "Cardinal Avery Dulles," in *Portraits: Popes, Family and Friends* (Brisbane, Australia/Leominster, Herefordshire: Connor Court/Gracewing, 2019), 185–89.

3. Carey, "Dulles, Avery," 245.

4. Carey, "Dulles, Avery," 246.

5. In *America* magazine for October 23, 1971, Leo J. O'Donovan, SJ, reported the conference.

6. For the text, see Robert J. Russell et al., eds., *Physics, Philosophy, and Theology: A Common Quest for Understanding* (Vatican City: Libreria Editrice Vaticana, 1988), 1–14. On the work of American and other Jesuits who have staffed the Vatican Observatory, see Guy Consolmagno, "Astronomy," *CEJ*, 67–68. In 1888, an Austrian Jesuit astronomer, Johann Hagen (1847–1930), became the director of the observatory program at Georgetown University; in 1904 he was appointed director of the Vatican Observatory; since 1934, the staffing of the Vatican Observatory has been entrusted to the Jesuit Order.

7. On Stoeger, see Denis Edwards, "Towards a Theology of Divine Action: William R. Stoeger on the Laws of Nature," *TS* 76 (2015): 485–502; Stephen J. Pope, "Does Evolution Have a Purpose? The Theological Significance of William Stoeger's Account of 'Nested Directionality,'" *TS* 78 (2016): 462–82; and Julia Feder, "Directed towards Relationship: William Stoeger's Immanent Directionality and Edward Schillebeeckx's Mystical Eschatology," *TS* 78 (2017): 447–61.

8. Ted Peters, et al., eds., *Resurrection: Theological and Scientific Assessments* (Grand Rapids, MI: Eerdmans, 2002); on this book, see G. O'Collins, *Believing in the Resurrection* (Mahwah, NJ: Paulist Press, 2012), 10–12.

9. See Peter Joseph Fritz, "Rahner, Karl, SJ," *CEJ*, 661–66.

10. In "Thursdays with Rahner," Kevin F. O'Brien, SJ, vividly recalls being taught Rahner's theology by Dych: *America*, May 3, 2004. See the exceptional article by O'Donovan, "A Journey into Time: The Legacy of Karl Rahner's Last Years," *TS* 46 (1985): 621–46.

11. Jacques Monet, SJ, and Frederick Crowe, SJ, "Lonergan, Bernard J., SJ," *CEJ*, 475–76.

12. In *On the Left Bank of the Tiber* (Brisbane, Australia/Leominster, UK: Connor Court/Gracewing, 2013), G. O'Collins recalls one group of American bishops whose updating course coincided with the cruelly short pontificate of John Paul I in 1978 (124–29).

13. During their time as deans of theology, two Americans, Francis A. Sullivan, SJ (dean 1964–70), and Jared Wicks, SJ (dean 1991–97), also carried forward reforms in the light of Vatican II.

14. On Jesuit input into ecclesiology, from the beginning to the present, see Susan K. Wood, "Ecclesiology," *CEJ*, 259–60. While also

including valuable entries on "catechism," "ecumenism, Jesuits and," "ethics," "fundamental theology," "grace," "justice," "liberation theology," "liturgy," and "theology," the *CEJ* has no entries on "Christology," "creation," "eschatology," "faith," "pastoral theology," "patristics," "sacraments," "sin," and "Trinity."

15. See Francis A. Sullivan, "Vatican II on the Charisms of the Faithful," in *Vatican II: Forty Personal Stories*, ed. William Madges and Michael J. Daley (Mystic, CT: Twenty-Third Publications, 2003), 94–97.

16. In *Theological Studies*, Sullivan often examined the question of the doctrinal weight of magisterial pronouncements (in 1994, 1995, 1997, 2002, 2003, 2012, and 2014).

17. "Teaching Authority Since Vatican II," *TS* 79 (2012): 570–89, at 587; "The Definitive Exercise of Teaching Authority," *TS* 75 (2014): 502–14, at 507–13.

18. See "The Significance of the Vatican II Declaration that the Church of Christ 'Subsists' in the Roman Catholic Church," in *Vatican II: Assessment and Perspectives: Twenty-Five Years After, 1962–87*, ed. R. Latourelle, vol. 2 (New York: Paulist Press, 1989), 272–87; an article in *TS* 67 (2006) that responded to Karl J. (later Cardinal) Becker, SJ, of the CDF, and articles in *TS* 69 (2008) and *TS* 71 (2010).

19. See also G. O'Collins, *From Rome to Royal Park* (Brisbane, Australia/Leominster, Herefordshire: Connor Court/Gracewing, 2015), 88, 180–88.

20. Paul Begheyn, SJ, "Fransen, Piet, SJ," *CEJ*, 314.

21. See G. O'Collins, *The Second Vatican Council on Other Religions* (Oxford: Oxford University Press, 2013), 109–11.

22. See Patrick J. Howell, SJ, "Burghardt, Walter, J.," *CEJ*, 125–26; James J. Martin, SJ, "Walter J. Burghardt," *America*, February 19, 2008.

23. *The Apostolic Fathers*, the very first volume for The Fathers of the Church, was translated by a team of three who included two Jesuits. From 1998, Lienhard has belonged to the editorial board of that series; in 2011 he was joined on the board by Brian Daley.

24. See G. O'Collins, "Grillmeier, Aloys, Cardinal, SJ," *CEJ*, 349–50.

25. Daley contributed a chapter on early Christian views of redemption in Christ to S. T. Davis, D. Kendall, and G. O'Collins, eds., *The Redemption* (Oxford: Oxford University Press, 2004), 149–76.

26. See Catherine E. Clifford, "Style Is Substance: Origins of John W. O'Malley's Contribution to the Interpretation of Vatican II," *TS* 20 (2018): 745–60.

27. Schloesser, "Against Forgetting: Memory, History, Vatican II," *TS* 67 (2006): 275–319; Ormerod, "'The Times They Are A'Changin'": A Response to O'Malley and Schloesser," *TS* 67 (2006): 834–55.

CHAPTER 4

1. See Eric Marcelo O. Genilo, SJ, "Ethics," *CEJ*, 288–89.

2. See Peter McDonough, *Men Astutely Trained: A History of the Jesuits in the American Century* (New York: The Free Press, 1992), 168–202, 295–318. The work of the ISO was, however, rendered less effective by the lack of Jesuit sociologists; among the first was Joseph H. Fichter (1908–94), who received a Harvard PhD in sociology in 1947; see Raymond A. Schroth, *The American Jesuits: A History* (New York: New York University Press, 2007), 147–54, 157–59.

3. McDonough, *Men Astutely Trained*, 182–83; Schroth, *The American Jesuits*, 128–30; see also Justin Poché, "Civil Rights Movement (United States)," *CEJ*, 170–72.

4. See David Schindler and Nicholas J. Healy, *Freedom, Truth, and Human Dignity: The Second Vatican Council's Declaration on Religious Freedom* (Grand Rapids, MI: Eerdmans, 2015).

5. See Yves Congar, *My Journal of the Council*, trans. Mary John Ronayne and Maria Cecily Boulding (Collegeville, MN: Liturgical Press, 2012), 734, 736, 803, and 834. On Murray, see McDonough, *Men Astutely Trained*, 214–41; William A. Clark, SJ, "Murray, John Courtney, SJ," *CEJ*, 535–36; and J. Leon Hooper, SJ, "John Courtney Murray's Societies," in *Major Jesuit Thinkers*, ed. Janez Perčič and Johannes Hergsell (Paderborn: Verlag Ferdinand Schöningh, 2018), 63–76.

6. McDonough, *Men Astutely Trained*, 227.

7. See Albert R. Jonsen and Stephen Toulmin, *The Abuse of Casuistry: A History of Moral Reasoning* (Oakland: University of California Press, 1990).

8. Bruges: Desclée de Brouwer, 1951.

9. See Eric Marcelo O. Genilo, SJ, "Ford, John Cuthbert, SJ," *CEJ*, 301–2; Aaron Pidel, "Ford's Foundation: The Consistency and

Compassion of a Pastoral Theologian," *America*, March 13, 2014, 25–28. See James F. Keenan, SJ, *A History of Catholic Moral Theology in the Twentieth Century: From Confessing Sins to Liberating Consciences* (London: Continuum, 2010); and Keenan, "Special Topic: Vatican II and Theological Ethics," *TS* 75 (2013): 162–90. On Lisa Sowle Cahill, Ford, Josef Fuchs, Keenan, Richard McCormick, and others, see Charles Curran, *Diverse Voices in Modern US Moral Theology* (Washington, DC: Georgetown University Press, 2019). On Fuchs, see James Keenan, "Fuchs, Josef, SJ," *CEJ*, 315–17.

10. *TS* 5 (1944): 261–309. Arthur Harris, appointed to lead Bomber Command in February 1942, was a fanatical believer in Area Bombing, fearfully demonstrated in the first thousand-bomber raid on Cologne, the firestorm that destroyed civilian Hamburg, and the obliteration of Dresden.

11. *TS* 39 (1978): 258–312.

12. Paulinus Ikechukwu Ochozor, *Richard A. McCormick and the Renewal of Moral Theology* (Notre Dame, IN: University of Notre Dame Press, 1995), 185–86.

13. See J. Keenan, ed., *Catholic Theological Ethics in the World Church: The Plenary Papers from the First Cross-Cultural Conference on Catholic Theological Ethics* [in Padua] (New York: Continuum, 2008); Keenan, "What Happened at Trento 2010," *TS* 72 (2011): 131–49.

14. "Making Sense of Eighty Years of Theological Ethics," *TS* 80 (2019): 157–68.

15. See Mark S. Massa, SJ, *The Structure of Theological Revolutions: How the Fight over Birth Control Transformed American Catholicism* (New York: Oxford University Press, 2018).

16. *TS* 47 (1986): 3–31, at 30n97.

17. See also Chan, "Biblical Ethics. 3D," *TS* 76 (2015): 112–28; and Chan, ed., *The Bible and Catholic Theological Ethics* (Maryknoll, NY: Orbis Books, 2018).

18. See Clare Robertson, "Gesù, Rome," *CEJ*, 335–37; Thomas Lucas, SJ, "Baroque Art and Architecture," *CEJ*, 82–87; William P. O'Brien, SJ, "Sacred Heart," *CEJ*, 704–5.

19. See Joanne M. Pierce, "Jungmann, Josef Andreas, SJ," *CEJ*, 352–54; for a general picture, Pierce, "Liturgy," *CEJ*, 473–74. When an international, professional association of Jesuit specialists in liturgy came into existence in 2004 at a meeting in Bangkok, almost inevitably they

called themselves the Jungmann Society. They hold biannual congresses: for instance, Dublin (2016) and Nairobi (2018).

20. Baldovin and his colleagues (who included Pecklers) supplied valuable material for G. O'Collins with John Wilkins, *Lost in Translation: The English Language and the Catholic Mass* (Collegeville, MN: Liturgical Press, 2017).

21. Charles Jurgensmeier, SJ, "Gelineau, Joseph, SJ," *CEJ*, 325–26. On Willcock, see Félix Zabala Lana, *Músicos Jesuitas: a lo largo de la historia* (Bilbao: Ediciones Mensajero, 2008), 79–81. This book also contains ample information on American Jesuit musicians: the Saint Louis Jesuits (Robert Dufford, John Foley, Roc O'Connor, and Dan Schutte), composers and performers; T. Frank Kennedy, musicologist and educator; C. J. McNaspy, musicologist and writer; and Kevin Waters, composer and educator. See also Charles Jurgensmeier, SJ, "Saint Louis Jesuits," *CEJ*, 705–6.

22. "Addai and Mari, Liturgy of," in *The Oxford Dictionary of the Christian Church*, ed. F. L. Cross and E. A. Livingstone, 3rd rev. ed. (Oxford: Oxford University Press, 2005), 17.

23. *Crux*, November 4, 2018.

24. See Paul A. Janowiak, SJ, "Preaching," *CEJ*, 640–45.

25. See Thomas Worcester, SJ, "Catechism," *CEJ*, 145–47.

26. José Alberto Mesa, SJ, "Nativity School Model," and "Cristo Rey (Model of Schools)," *CEJ*, 551–52, 208–10.

27. Jorge Salcedo, SJ, "Fe y Alegría," *CEJ*, 295–96.

28. Genilo, "Ford, John," 302.

29. Keith Maczkiewicz, SJ, "Jesuit Refugee Service (JRS)," *CEJ*, 419–20.

30. Keith Maczkiewicz, "Lord, Daniel, SJ," *CEJ*, 476–77.

31. Pedro Arrupe, the superior general of the Society of Jesus, visited Berrigan during his imprisonment.

32. Rahner understood pastoral (he called it "practical") theology to be the self-realization of the Church; see his *Theological Investigations*, vol. 9 (London: Darton, Longman & Todd, 1972), 101–14.

33. See Robert J. Kaslyn, SJ, "Canon Law and the Society of Jesus," *CEJ*, 134–36.

34. Thomas Massaro, SJ, "Drinan, Robert F., SJ," *CEJ*, 242–43.

35. Carroll, *JCP*, vol. 1, 46: "When the ministers of religion leave the duties of their profession to take a busy part in political matters,

they generally fall into contempt; and sometimes even bring discredit to the cause, in whose service they are engaged."

36. Massaro, "Drinan," 242.

37. L. Orsy, *Receiving the Council: Theological and Canonical Insights and Debates* (Collegeville, MN: Liturgical Press, 2009), 91–104.

38. See *Origins* 28, no. 8 (July 16, 1998): 113–16; Orsy did the translation (from Latin into English) of this apostolic letter. The same issue of *Origins* carried the English translation of a commentary by Ratzinger (116–19).

39. London *Tablet*, June 17, 2010.

40. *TS* 31 (1970): 243–61.

41. Jon Sobrino, SJ, "Jesus of Nazareth from the Salvadoran Context: Compassion, Hope, and Following the Light of the Cross," *TS* 70 (2009): 437–70; Phillip E. Berryman, "Latin American Liberation Theology," *TS* 34 (1973): 357–95; Michael L. Cook, SJ, "Jesus from the Other Side of History: Christology in Latin America," *TS* 44 (1983): 258–97; Alfred T. Hennelly, SJ, "The Challenge of Juan Luis Segundo," *TS* 38 (1977): 125–35; Alfred T. Hennelly, SJ, "Theological Method: The Southern Exposure," *TS* 38 (1977): 709–35; Joyce Murray, "Liberation for Communion in the Soteriology of Gustavo Gutiérrez," *TS* 59 (1998): 51–59; James B. Nickoloff, "Church of the Poor: The Ecclesiology of Gustavo Gutiérrez," *TS* 54 (1993): 512–35; T. Howland Sanks, SJ, and Brian H. Smith, SJ, "Liberation Theology: Praxis, Theory, Praxis," *TS* 38 (1977): 3–38; T. Howland Sanks, SJ, "Liberation Theology and the Social Gospel: Variations on the Theme," *TS* 41 (1980): 668–82. See also J. Matthew Ashley, "Ignacio Ellacuría and the Spiritual Exercises of Ignatius Loyola," *TS* 61 (2000): 16–39; Peter C. Phan, "Method in Liberation Theologies," *TS* 61 (2000): 40–63.

42. Gutiérrez ("The Option for the Poor Arises from Faith in Christ" [*TS* 70 (2009): 317–326]), and Sobrino ("Jesus of Galilee from the Salvadoran Context" [*TS* 70 (2009): 437–460]).

43. See Matthew T. Eggemeier, "Liberation Theology, Latin American," *CEJ*, 464–69; Kevin F. Burke, SJ, "Ellacuría, Ignacio, SJ (1930–89) and Companions," *CEJ*, 275–80.

44. Rosemary Radford Ruether, "Paradoxes of Human Hope: The Messianic Horizon of Church and Society," *TS* 33 (1972): 235–52.

45. *TS* 36 (1975).

CHAPTER 5

1. See Romeo de Maio, *The Book of the Gospels at the Oecumenical Councils* (Vatican City: Biblioteca Apostolica Vaticana, 1963). For help toward the making of this chapter, we thank very warmly Brendan Byrne, SJ, and Richard Clifford, SJ. The responsibility for the final text is, of course, our own.

2. See J. M. Lera, "Sacrae paginae studium sit veluti anima Sacrae Theologiae: Notas sobre el origen y procedencia de esta frase," in *Palabra y Vida*, ed. A. Vargas Machuca and Gregorio Ruiz (Madrid: Universidad Comillas, 1984), 409–22.

3. See "Maldonado, Juan," in *The Oxford Dictionary of the Christian Church*, ed. F. L. Cross and E. A. Livingstone, 3rd rev. ed. (Oxford: Oxford University Press, 2005), 1030.

4. See Alice L. Laffey, "Lapide, Cornelius a, SJ," *CEJ*, 456–57; Laffey, "Biblical Studies," *CEJ*, 96–101; see also "Cornelius a Lapide," *Oxford Dictionary of the Christian Church*, 422.

5. For the general background, Donald Senior, "The Bible and Catholicism," in *The Oxford Handbook of the Bible in America*, ed. Paul C. Gutjahr (Oxford: Oxford University Press, 2018), 517–30.

6. See Gerald Fogarty, *American Catholic Biblical Scholarship: A History from the Early Republic to Vatican II* (San Francisco: Harper & Row, 1989), 3–4.

7. On Maas, see Fogarty, *American Catholic Biblical Scholarship*, 40–44.

8. Fogarty, *American Catholic Biblical Scholarship*, 79–82.

9. Fogarty, *American Catholic Biblical Scholarship*, 80.

10. On Drum, see Fogarty, *American Catholic Biblical Scholarship*, 180–83, 188–91.

11. On Billot, see Fogarty, *American Catholic Biblical Scholarship*, 171–73.

12. See G. O'Collins, *Inspiration: Towards a Christian Interpretation of Biblical Inspiration* (Oxford: Oxford University Press, 2018), 118–23.

13. See Fogarty, *American Catholic Biblical Scholarship*, 45.

14. Fogarty, *American Catholic Biblical Scholarship*, 99; for a fuller account of the negative impact of the Biblical Commission and *Pascendi*, see 140–70.

15. See Fogarty, *American Catholic Biblical Scholarship*, 58–77; Raymond A. Schroth, *The American Jesuits: History* (New York: New York University Press, 2007), 95–96.

16. See Laffey, "Pontifical Biblical Institute (PIB/PBI)," *CEJ*, 628–30.

17. See Fogarty, *American Catholic Biblical Scholarship*, 198.

18. See Mary Ann Hinsdale, "Bea, Augustin, Cardinal, SJ," *CEJ*, 87–89.

19. See Fogarty, *American Catholic Biblical Scholarship*, 240.

20. See Donald Senior, *Raymond E. Brown and the Catholic Biblical Renewal* (Mahwah, NJ: Paulist Press, 2018), 80–81. Brown, Fitzmyer, and Murphy also served as editors of the *New Jerome Biblical Commentary* (1989), for which Cardinal Carlo Maria Martini, like Bea, a rector of the Pontifical Biblical Institute, wrote the foreword.

21. For the history of the CBA, see also Francis S. Rossiter and Joseph Jensen, *Catholic Biblical Quarterly*, 66 Supplement (2004): 1–16.

22. In 1955, the CBA was to produce a Festschrift in honor of O'Hara, who had done so much toward founding and developing the association. In 1992, Cardinal Timothy Dolan published a life of O'Hara, *Some Seed Fell on Good Ground* (Washington, DC: Catholic University of America).

23. On Abbott, see James Martin, SJ, *America* magazine, March 5, 2008. Simon ("Si") E. Smith, SJ (b. 1930), a member of the first team of "abstracters" for *NTA*, informed O'Collins that "the idea" of creating *NTA* in 1956 was "entirely Walter Abbott's. But protocol required that a faculty priest be listed as editor. So John Collins was listed as editor-in-chief." The real founder and first editor was, however, Abbott.

24. See Alice L. Laffey, "MacRae, George W., SJ," *CEJ*, 492. From 1973, MacRae began teaching at Harvard Divinity School; at the time of his death, he had just begun an appointment as acting dean of Harvard Divinity School.

25. One of the few Bible institutes left is located at College Misericordia, Dallas, PA (founded in 1924 by the Sisters of Mercy and renamed in 2007 Misericordia University). Its one-week summer school in Sacred Scripture is now into its fifty-first year. MacRae encouraged O'Collins to start publishing with the *CBQ*, and the encouragement had quick results: "Power Made Perfect in Weakness: 2 Cor 12:9–10," *CBQ* 33 (1971): 528–37.

26. *Bulletin of the American Schools of Oriental Research* 134 (April 1954): 3–4, at 4. O'Callaghan came to Albright after studying at the Gregorian University (1936–40). He finished his PhD at Johns Hopkins in 1946 (with a superb thesis published as *Aram Naharaim*), taught at the Biblicum in Rome, engaged in archaeological digs, and left on a Fulbright scholarship for Iraq in July 1953. The following March 5, he died on a stormy night outside Baghdad, when the car in which he was traveling crashed into a broken-down truck left standing on the road without lights. Aram Naharaim (also called Haran, e.g., in Gen 11:31) is the biblical name for a region of Upper Mesopotamia bordering on the Euphrates. Unlike O'Callaghan and others, some American Jesuits like Richard J. Clifford (b. 1934) and Daniel Harrington studied in the Near Eastern Languages and Literature (NELL) program, later renamed Near Eastern Languages and Civilizations (NELC), at Harvard. Yet even there they were taught by an outstanding student of Albright and top expert on the Dead Sea Scrolls, Frank Moore Cross (1921–2012).

27. Fogarty, *American Catholic Biblical Scholarship*, 234.

28. He published a spin-off article, "Dead Sea Scrolls: Thanksgiving Psalms," in *TS* 13 (1952): 487–524.

29. Another Canadian Jesuit, Michael F. Kolarcik (b. 1950), who was also a distinguished Old Testament scholar, would be appointed rector of the Biblicum in 2014.

30. For details, Fogarty, *American Catholic Biblical Scholarship*, 281–310. For a picture of Fenton's ranting and ugly behavior at a preconciliar meeting in Rome of March 8, 1962, see Yves Congar, *My Diary of the Council*, trans. Mary John Ronayne and Mary Cecily Boulding (Collegeville, MN: Liturgical Press, 2012): "Fenton was so hateful, so obstinately negative, so aggressive, so utterly senseless, that Mgr. [Gérard] Philips got up and said, with emotion, but forcefully and calmly, 'It is impossible to work in these conditions and I am leaving. Because (turning to Fenton)—you accuse everyone of heresy. It is impossible to work unless one respects others and their points of view.' Fenton was quiet for a while and then began again. He is out of his senses and beyond all reasonable control" (77).

31. See John M. Oesterreicher, "Declaration on the Relationship of the Church to Non-Christian Religions," in *Commentary on the Documents of Vatican II*, ed. Herbert Vorgrimler, trans. Simon and Erika Young and Hilda Graef, vol. 3 (London: Burns & Oates, 1969), 1–136, at 8–9. For the text of Vogt's submission, see *Acta et Documenta*

Concilio Oecumenico Vatican II Apparando, I/IV/I, 1 (Vatican City: Typis Polyglottis Vaticanis, 1961), 131–34.

32. Later, two American Jesuits were to be appointed rectors of the Biblicum: Robert F. O'Toole (rector 1996–2002) and Stephen F. Pisano (rector 2002–8). Both contributed to the monumental *Anchor Bible Dictionary*, 6 vols. (1992), as did Thomas Tobin, SJ (see later in this chapter). O'Toole was a specialist on Luke/Acts. For many years Pisano taught text criticism, as well as working on the revision of the (Latin) Vulgate translation of the OT. In 1995 the final (eighteenth) volume of a revised edition of the OT appeared.

33. From 1979, North was to compile the valuable *Elenchus bibliographicus biblicus*, renamed the *Elenchus of Biblical Bibliography*.

34. The following year, this article was distributed to bishops assembled for Vatican II, along with a pamphlet published (in English, French, German, and Spanish) by the Biblicum itself: "A New Attack against Catholic Exegesis and against the Pontifical Biblical Institute." Étienne Fouilloux puts the Lateran offensive in a wide context: "The Antepreparatory Phase," in *History of Vatican II*, ed. Giuseppe Alberigo and Joseph A. Komonchak, vol. 1 (Maryknoll, NY: Orbis Books, 1995), 55–166, at 138–40.

35. Fogarty, *American Catholic Biblical Scholarship*, 322–25.

36. Mahwah, NJ: Paulist Press.

37. (Oxford: Oxford University Press, 2018), 166–94.

38. O'Collins, *Inspiration*, 62–86.

39. In an online article reported by Donald Senior, *Raymond E. Brown and the Catholic Biblical Renewal*, 281, Gignac gives an account of the revision: "The Revision of the New Testament of the New American Bible."

40. Clifford told the ugly story in *America* magazine, May 22, 1995. In that article he invited the U.S. bishops to insist on their ratification of the entire revised NAB, but they failed to do so. The way became open for something worse—the Vatican takeover of the English-speaking Missal. In 1998 a skillfully revised translation of the Roman Missal, eminently suitable for proclamation and approved by all eleven English-speaking conferences of bishops (including the American conference), was dismissed without discussion. The International Committee on English in the Liturgy (ICEL) was then dismantled, and a clumsy, Latinized "translation" was introduced in 2010. On all of this, see Gerald O'Collins with John Wilkins, *Lost in Translation: The English Language and the Catholic*

Mass (Collegeville, MN: Liturgical Press, 2017). The odd guidelines (*Liturgiam Authenticam*), which eventually produced the 2010 translation of the Missal, were sharply criticized by Clifford in the *CBQ* 63 (2001): 197–202.

CHAPTER 6

1. G. O'Collins, *From Rome to Royal Park* (Brisbane: Connor Court, 2015), 14–16.

2. Grégoire Catta, SJ, "Dictionnaire de Spiritualité," *CEJ*, 232.

3. Joseph P. Chinnici, "Organization of the Spiritual Life: American Catholic Devotional Works 1791–1866," *TS* 40 (1979): 229–55.

4. See Jared Wicks, SJ, "Scripture Reading Urged *Vehementer* (DV No. 25): Background and Development," *TS* 73 (2013): 555–80.

5. See Keith F. Pecklers, SJ, *The Unread Vision: The Liturgical Movement in the United States of America 1926–1955* (Collegeville, MN: Liturgical Press, 1998); Pecklers, "Liturgical Movement, Catholic," *The New Catholic Encyclopedia*, vol. 8 (Washington, DC: Catholic University of America Press, 2003), 670–76, at 674–76.

6. See *Worship* 37 (1963): 330, 373.

7. Ellard also published articles on the liturgy in the Jesuit quarterly *Theological Studies*: e.g., two in *TS* 21 (1960).

8. See Gabriel Flynn and Paul Murray, eds., *Ressourcement: A Movement for Renewal in Twentieth-Century Catholic Theology* (Oxford: Oxford University Press, 2012).

9. See John Gavin, SJ, "Iparraguirre, Ignacio, SJ," *CEJ*, 403–4.

10. See Philip Endean, SJ, "Spiritual Exercises," *CEJ*, 757–62.

11. Henry Shea, SJ, "Discernment," *CEJ*, 234–35; Shea, "Spirits, Good and Evil," *CEJ*, 757.

12. See Brian O'Leary, SJ, "Examen," *CEJ*, 290–91.

13. Thomas Worcester, SJ, "Direction, Spiritual," *CEJ*, 232–34.

14. Eastern Point is the only retreat house in the United States where the primary work is giving the Exercises on a one-to-one basis in eight- and thirty-day retreats.

15. Keith Maczkiewicz, SJ, "Ignatian Spirituality Centers," *CEJ*, 375–77. The first Jesuit retreat house in the United States that was

intended for private as well as preached retreats opened in 1911, Mount Manresa Jesuit Retreat House in Staten Island. In 2013, it closed, and its ministry moved to St. Mary of the Assumption Parish.

16. Henry Shea, SJ, "Institute of Jesuit Sources/Institute for Advanced Jesuit Studies," *CEJ*, 396–97.

17. *The American Jesuits: A History* (New York: New York University Press, 2007), 206–8.

18. *TS* 77 (2016): 118–35.

19. *TS* 77 (2016): 905–21.

20. Keenan also coedited Amoris Laetitia*: A New Momentum for Moral Formation and Pastoral Practice* (Mahwah, NJ: Paulist Press, 2018).

CHAPTER 7

1. On the Council and its achievements, see Giuseppe Alberigo and Joseph A. Komonchak, eds., *History of Vatican II*, 5 vols. (Maryknoll, NY: Orbis Books, 1995–2006); Yves Congar et al., eds., *L'Église et Vatican II*, 3 vols. (Paris: Cerf, 1966–67); up to 1970, twenty-one further volumes appeared in this series of commentaries on the Council's documents; Peter Hünermann and Jochen Hilberath, eds., *Herders Theologischer Kommentar zum Zweiten Vatikanischen Konzil*, 5 vols. (Freiburg im Breisgau: Herder, 2004–5); Gerald O'Collins, *The Second Vatican Council: Message and Meaning* (Collegeville, MN: Liturgical Press, 2014); John W. O'Malley, *What Happened at Vatican II* (Cambridge, MA: Belknap Press of Harvard University Press, 2008); Herbert Vorgrimler, ed., *Commentary on the Documents of Vatican II*, 5 vols. (London: Burns & Oates, 1967–69; German orig. 1966–68).

2. See G. O'Collins, "Vatican II, Jesuits and," *CEJ*, 518–20; and O'Collins, "Does the Second Vatican Council Represent Continuity or Discontinuity?" *The Second Vatican Council*, 25–56.

3. See Alberto Melloni (director), *Vatican II: The Complete History* (Mahwah, NJ: Paulist Press, 2015), 174–81, 192–97; Radu Bordeianu, "Orthodox Observers at the Second Vatican Council and Intra-Orthodox Dynamics," *TS* 79 (2018): 86–106; Mauro Velati, *Separati ma Fratelli: Gli osservatori non cattolici al Vaticano II (1962–1965)* (Bologna: Il Mulino, 2014).

4. On the contribution Jesuits made to Vatican II, see G. O'Collins, "Vatican II, Jesuits and," *CEJ*, 518–20; and Mary Ann Hinsdale, "Periti," *CEJ*, 600–602.

5. Küng describes his American tour in *My Struggle for Freedom* (Grand Rapids, MI: Eerdmans, 2003), 302–18.

6. *TS* 25 (1964): 197–216.

7. Stanley, "The New Testament Basis," 213.

8. See Karl Rahner, SJ, "Dogmatic Constitution on the Church," in *Commentary on the Documents of Vatican II*, vol. 1, 195–205; Joseph Ratzinger, "Announcement and Prefatory Notes of Explanation," in *Commentary on the Documents of Vatican II*, vol. 1, 297–305; Joseph A. Komonchak, "Episcopacy and Collegiality," in *History of Vatican II*, vol. 4, 62–86; Alberto Melloni, "The Debate on Collegiality," in *History of Vatican II*, vol. 3, 64–105; Luis Antonio G. Tagle, "The *Nota Explicativa Previa*," in *History of Vatican II*, vol. 4, 417–45.

9. *Acta Apostolicae Sedis* 56 (1964): 712–18.

10. "The Biblical Commission's Instruction on the Historical Truth of the Gospels," *TS* 25 (1964): 386–408, at 387; note 19, 398, shows how Fitzmyer was aware that the instruction could contribute to what became Vatican II's constitution, *Dei Verbum*.

11. *TS* 22 (1961): 426–44.

12. *TS* 25 (1964): 503–75.

13. *TS* 27 (1966): 580–606. On *Dignitatis Humanae*, see Silvia Scatena, *La fatica della libertà: l'elaborazione della dichiarazione* "Dignitatis Humanae" *sulla libertà del Vaticano II* (Bologna: Il Mulino, 2003); O'Collins, *The Second Vatican Council*, 35–40.

14. See Dennis M. Linehan, SJ, "Of Many Things," *America*, February 26, 2007.

15. *TS* 28 (1967): 683–705.

16. *TS* 29 (1968): 37–51.

17. *TS* 28 (1967): 733–48, at 747–48.

18. *TS* 28 (1967): 733–48, at 747–48.

19. David Hollenbach, "Nuclear Weapons and Nuclear War: The Shape of the Catholic Debate," *TS* 43 (1982): 577–605.

20. Drew Christiansen, "On Relative Equality: Catholic Egalitarianism after Vatican II," *TS* 45 (1984): 651–75.

21. *TS* 70 (2009): 751–81.

22. *TS* 70 (2009): 874–903.

23. *TS* 27 (1966): 179–203.

24. *TS* 28 (1967): 51–75.

25. *TS* 29 (1968): 191–214.

26. *TS* 36 (1975): 493–502; Kathleen Duffy wrote a long entry, "Teilhard de Chardin, Pierre, SJ," for *CEJ*, 774–80, but did not mention the influence of Teilhard at Vatican II.

27. S. Schloesser, "Against Forgetting: Memory, History, and Vatican II," in *Vatican II: Did Anything Happen?* ed. David G. Schultenover, SJ (New York: Continuum, 2007), 92–152, at 123.

28. *TS* 32 (1971): 573–601.

29. *TS* 44 (1983): 373–406; *TS* 67 (2006): 3–33.

30. "Priesthood, Ministry, and Religious Life: Some Historical and Historiographical Considerations," *TS* 49 (1988): 223–57.

31. *TS* 33 (1972): 199–234.

32. *TS* 34 (1973): 643–78.

33. *TS* 30 (1969): 289–311; *TS* 41 (1980): 253–302; *TS* 44 (1983): 3–29.

34. J. Wicks, *Man Yearning for Grace: Luther's Early Spiritual Teaching* (Washington, DC: Corpus Books, 1968); J. Wicks, ed., *Catholic Scholars Dialogue with Luther* (Chicago: Loyola University Press, 1970); J. Wicks, *Luther and His Spiritual Legacy* (Wilmington, DE: Michael Glazier, 1984).

35. For the pontificate of John Paul II (1978–2005), see J. Wicks, "John Paul II and Lutherans: Actions and Reactions," in *The Legacy of John Paul II*, ed. G. O'Collins and Michael A. Hayes (London: Burns & Oates, 2008), 139–202. On the wider story of Jesuit involvement in ecumenical activity, see Michael A. Fahey, SJ, "Ecumenism, Jesuits and," *CEJ*, 265–71.

36. *TS* 40 (1979): 716–27. Further treatment of this theme is found in K. Rahner, *Theological Investigations* 20 (London: Darton, Longman & Todd, 1981), 77–102.

37. T. Howland Sanks, SJ, "Education for Ministry Since Vatican II," *TS* 45 (1984): 481–500.

38. See Giuseppe Alberigo and James Provost, eds., *Synod 1985: An Evaluation* (Edinburgh: T. & T. Clark, 1986).

39. A. Dulles, "The Reception of Vatican II and the Extraordinary Synod of 1985," in *The Reception of Vatican II*, ed. Giuseppe Alberigo, Jean Pierre Jossua, and Joseph A. Komonchak (Washington, DC: Catholic University of America Press, 1987), 349–63; A. Dulles, *Vatican II and the Extraordinary Synod: An Overview* (Collegeville, MN: Liturgical Press, 1986).

40. Mahwah, NJ: Paulist Press, 1988–89.

41. He served as editor from 1985 to 2002.

42. Maryknoll, NY: Orbis Books, 1995–2006.

43. G. O'Collins, *Retrieving Fundamental Theology* (Mahwah, NJ: Paulist Press, 1993), 178–217; the bibliography was prepared with Joseph Cassar, SJ.

44. *TS* 62 (2001): 231–61; *TS* 69 (2008): 3–37; *TS* 71 (2010): 609–36.

45. *TS* 72 (2011): 586–619.

46. *TS* 37 (1976): 545–66.

47. (Maryknoll, NY: Orbis Books), 183, 184.

48. London: Geoffrey Chapman, 1992.

49. *TS* 56 (1995): 521–50.

50. *TS* 51 (1990): 268–85; see also his "Hindu Views of Religious Others: Implications for Christian Theology," *TS* 64 (2003): 306–33.

51. *TS* 56 (1995): 521–50.

52. On Clooney and other Jesuits who found in *Nostra Aetate* a rich point of departure for their interreligious ministry and scholarship, see Michael Barnes, SJ, "Interreligious Dialogue," *CEJ*, 398–403.

53. *TS* 75 (2014): 847–62; reprinted in J. Wicks, *Investigating Vatican II: Its Theologians, Ecumenical Turn, and Biblical Commitment* (Washington, DC: Catholic University of America Press, 2018), 11–30.

54. "Vatican II on Revelation—Behind the Scenes," *TS* 71 (2010): 637–50; reprinted in Wicks, *Investigating Vatican II*, 80–97.

55. Reprinted in Wicks, *Investigating Vatican II*, 31–79.

56. J. Wicks, "Joseph Ratzinger: Warming the Christic Imagination, October 1962," in *The Lord Jesus: Christocentric Essays in Honor of Robert P. Imbelli*, ed. Andrew Meszaros (Washington, DC: Catholic University of America Press, forthcoming). A shorter version of this article is published in *Gregorianum 101 (2020): 233–49*.

CONCLUSIONS

1. See Patrick W. Carey, "Feeney, Leonard," *CEJ*, 296–97; Raymond A. Schroth, SJ, *The American Jesuits: A History* (New York: New York University Press, 2007), 209–11.

INDEX OF NAMES

Abbott, Walter M., 18, 41, 77, 107, 137
Accolti, Michele, 14
Adams, Raymond A., 107–8
Aelred of Rievaulx, St., 12
Ahern, Barnabas M., 81
Alberigo, Giuseppe, 112, 139, 141, 143
Albright, William Foxwell, 78–80, 138
Allegro, John Marco, 17, 127
Allen, John, 59
Alonso-Schökel, Luis, xi, 77, 78
Amidon, Philip R., 45, 47
Anselm of Canterbury, St., 45
Antonelli, Cardinal Leonardo, 10
Aquinas, St. Thomas, viii, 9, 22–25, 27, 45, 53, 57
Arintero, J. G., 94
Aristotle, 21, 22
Arius, 51
Arrupe, Pedro, 54, 62, 134
Aschenbrenner, George A., 94–96
Ashley, J. Matthew, 135
Athanasius of Alexandria, St., 51
Augustine of Hippo, St., 16, 44–46
Autry, Gene, 50

Baldovin, John F., 58, 134
Balthasar, Hans Urs von, ix, 39
Bannwart, Clemens, 51
Barnes, Michael, 144
Barry, William A., xiii, 91, 95–96
Barth, Karl, 129
Basil the Great, St., 50
Baum, Gregory, 108–9
Bea, Cardinal Augustin, 76–77, 82, 91, 107, 137
Beauduin, Lambert, 92
Bechard, Dean P., 87
Becker, Karl Josef, Cardinal, 131
Begheyn, Paul, 131
Bellarmine, St. Robert, 11, 33, 60, 129
Bellitto, Christopher, xiii
Benedict XV, Pope, 23
Benedict XVI, Pope. *See* Ratzinger, Joseph
Benoit, Pierre, 81
Bergson, Henri, 24

Bernauer, James W., 128, 129
Berrigan, Daniel J., xi, 54, 63–64, 134
Berryman, Philip E., 135
Billot, Louis, 23, 74, 136
Blanchette, Oliva, 129
Blondel, Maurice, 24, 129
Bobadilla, Nicholas, 72
Bonachea, Rolando E., 128
Borchert, Donald M., 28
Bordeianu, Radu, 141
Borgia, St. Francis, 72
Borromeo, Cardinal Vitaliano, 4
Boulding, Mary Cecily, 132, 138
Bouscaren, Timothy Lincoln, 65
Boyle, Gregory J., 63
Boys, Mary C., 116
Bright, John, 78
Brodeur, Scott N., 87
Brough, John B., 128
Brown, Dorothy M., 127
Brown, Raymond E., xii, 38, 69, 77–78, 80, 137, 139
Brown, Robert McAfee, 5, 17, 104
Buber, Martin, 27
Buckley, Michael J., 35
Bullivant, Stephen, 113
Burghardt, Walter J., x, 15–16, 44–45, 60, 121, 127, 131
Burke, Kevin F., 69, 135
Byrne, Brendan, xiii, 99, 136

Cahill, Lisa Sowle, 57, 70, 133
Canisius, St. Peter, 60
Carey, Patrick W., 129, 130, 144
Carroll, Charles, 3
Carroll, Daniel, 2, 3
Carroll, John, Archbishop, viii, 1–8, 10, 58, 66, 73, 90, 123–25, 134–35
Caruana, Louis, xiii, 31
Casel, Odo, 92
Cassar, Joseph, 144
Cassem, Edwin ("Ned") H., 61
Catta, Grégoire, 140
Chadwick, Henry, 46
Chan, Yiu Sing Lúcás, 58, 133
Chinnici, Joseph P., 142
Christiansen, Drew J., 64–65, 100, 108, 142
Clark, William A., 127, 132
Clarke, W. Norris, x, 25, 27, 30, 120, 129
Clement XIII, Pope, 2
Clement XIV, Pope, 1, 2, 124
Clement of Alexandria, 43, 114
Clements, Charlotte, xiii
Clifford, Catherine E., 118, 132
Clifford, Richard J., xi, xiii, 35, 85–87, 136, 138, 139, 140
Clooney, Francis Xavier, 113, 115, 144
Coffin, William Sloane, 63
Collins, James D., 26
Collins, John J., 77, 86, 137
Cone, James H., 35
Congar, Yves, Cardinal, 15, 34, 44, 54, 81, 93, 103, 106, 113, 115, 132, 138, 141
Conley, John J., 30–31
Conn, James J., 65–66
Connolly, William J., 96
Consolmagno, Guy, 36, 49, 130
Coogan, Michael D., 83
Cook, Michael L., 39, 135
Cooke, Bernard J., 43, 58

Copleston, Frederick C., 28–31, 120, 129
Coppens, Charles, 11, 12
Cornille, Catherine, 70
Cowan, Marian, 95
Coyne, George V., 35, 49
Crilly, Donna, iv
Cross, F. L., 134, 136
Cross, Frank Moore, 138
Crouzel, Henri, 45
Crowe, Frederick, 129, 130
Crowley, Paul G., 117
Curran, Charles E., 133
Curran, R. Emmett, 5, 123, 124, 125, 126
Currie, Charles, 62, 64
Cushing, Richard, Cardinal, 120–21
Cyril of Alexandria, St., 16, 47

Dahood, Mitchell J., 79, 80, 82
Daley, Brian E., xiii, 36, 45–47, 49, 59, 120, 131
Daley, Michael J., 131
Daly, Claude R., 50
Daly, Robert J., 43
Daniélou, Cardinal Jean, 15–16, 34, 44, 45, 93, 104
D'Arcy, Martin, 24
Darwin, Charles, 31
Davis, Stephen T., iii, 36, 40, 46, 131
Day, Dorothy, xiii
De Concilio, Januarius Vincent, 11
DeGoia, John J., 122
De Guibert, Joseph, 94
De Lubac, Cardinal Henri, 15, 34, 45, 81, 93
De Maio, Romeo, 136
Demase, Isaac, xiii
De Mello, Anthony, iii, 94, 98
De Niro, Robert, 64
Denzinger, Heinrich, 51
De Smet, Peter John, 14, 128
Dezza, Cardinal Paolo, 18
Diekmann, Godfrey L., 92
Dinh, Hoa, xiii
Di Vito, Robert A., 83
Dodd, William H., 107
Doherty, Cathal, 129
Dolan, Cardinal Timothy, 137
Donahue, John R., 57–58, 87, 120
Dooley, P. J., 125, 126
Doran, Robert M., xiii, 30, 38
Doyle, Dennis M., 117
Drinan, Robert F., 66, 134, 135
Drum, Walter, 74, 136
Dufford, Robert J., 134
Duffy, Kathleen, 142
Dulles, Avery, Cardinal, x, 20–21, 34–35, 39–41, 49, 65, 100, 109–12, 129, 130, 143
Dunn, James D. G., 84
Dupuis, Jacques, iii, 40, 43, 112, 114, 144
Dych, William V., 37, 130
Dyson, Robert A., 82

Edwards, Denis, 130
Egan, Harvey D., 37
Eggemeier, Matthew T., 135
Ellacuría, Ignacio, 69, 135
Ellard, Gerald, 58, 92, 107, 149
Ellis, John Tracy, xiii, 48
Endean, Philip, 94, 140

Endres, John C., 87
Eslick, Leonard J., 26

Faggioli, Massimo, 118
Fahey, Michael A., 143
Faustus of Riez, 17
Fay, Maureen A., 122
Feder, Julia, 130
Feeney, Leonard, 120–22, 144
Feiner, Johannes, 54, 106
Fenton, Joseph Clifford, 81–82, 104, 117, 138
Fessio, Joseph, 39
Fichter, Joseph H., 132
Finn, Francis J., 11, 90
Fisichella, Rino, Archbishop, 39, 126
Fitzmyer, Joseph A., xi, 16–17, 60, 77, 79–80, 84, 86, 90–91, 104–7, 119–20, 127, 137, 142
Flannery, Kevin L., 31
Fleming, David L., 94, 96
Flynn, Gabriel, 140
Fogarty, Gerald P., 48, 112, 136, 137, 138, 139
Foley, John B., 134
Ford, John C., xi, 55–56, 62, 132–34
Forte, Anthony J., 87
Foster, David R., 128
Fouilloux, Étienne, 139
Francis, Pope, iv, xii, 54, 98–100, 117–18
Francis Xavier, St., x, 2
Franco, Francisco, 24
Franklin, Benjamin, 3, 4, 66
Fransen, Piet, 44, 131
Franzelin, Johann Baptist, Cardinal, 12, 75, 128
Fritz, Peter J., 130
Fuchs, Josef, 56, 133
Fulco, William J., 87
Fuller, Reginald H., 78
Furay, John B., ix
Futrell, John C., 95

Gallagher, Charles R., 48
Galileo, 31
Ganganelli, Lorenzo. *See* Clement XIV, Pope
Gannett, Cinthia, 125
Gannon, Robert I., 24
Ganss, George E., 97
Garaudy, Roger, 28
Garraghan, Gilbert J., 126
Gaston, William A., 29
Gavin, John, 128, 140
Geisinger, Robert J., 65–66
Gelineau, Joseph, 59, 134
Genicot, Eduard, 55
Genilo, Eric Marcelo O., 62, 132, 134
Gensler, Harry J., xiii, 30
Giblin, C. Homer, 86
Gibson, Mel, 87
Gignac, Francis T., 86, 139
Gill, James J., 61
Gilson, Étienne, 23, 27, 28
Giuliani, Maurice, 94
Glanzman, George S., 79, 80
Glyn, Justin, xiii
Gonzales, Zephyrinus, Cardinal, 23
Gortebecke, Albert, 55
Graef, Hilda, 138
Gregory of Nazianzus, St., 50
Gregory of Nyssa, St., 50
Gregory XVI, Pope, 9

Grillmeier, Cardinal Aloys, 46–47, 131
Grisez, Germain G., 56
Groppe, Elizabeth T., 113
Gruenthaner, Michael J., 77, 86
Guardini, Romano, 92
Guarino, Thomas G., 128
Guéranger, Prosper, 92
Guilday, Peter, 123
Guinness, Alec, 103–4
Gutiérrez, Gustavo, 69, 135
Gutjahr, Paul C., 136

Hagen, Johann, 130
Haight, Roger D., 39
Hallett, Garth L., 26
Hamm, Dennis M., 87
Hanley, Thomas O., xv, 123
Hardon, John A., 60
Harmless, William J., 45, 47
Harrington, Daniel J., xi, 77, 85–86, 91, 138
Harris, Arthur, 133
Hartshorne, Charles, 26
Hawking, Stephen, 49
Hayes, Michael A., 143
Healy, Nicholas J., 132
Hecker, Isaac, 76
Heelan, Patrick Aidan, 25, 28–29
Heft, James J., 114
Hegel, Georg W. F., 28
Heidegger, Martin, 28, 30, 129
Heisenberg, Werner, 28–29
Henle, Robert J., 26
Henn, William, 109
Hennelly, Alfred T., 135
Henry of Ghent, 45
Hergsell, Johannes, 132
Heschel, Abraham Joshua, 63
Hilberath, Jochen, 141
Hilbert, Michael P., 65
Hill, Richard A., 65
Hinsdale, Mary Ann, 125, 127, 128, 137, 142
Hoffmann, Manfred, 109
Hollenbach, David, 57, 108, 142
Hooper, J. Leon, xiii, 132
Howell, Patrick J., 127, 131
Hügel, Friedrich von, 13
Hughson, Thomas, 113
Hünermann, Peter, 141
Hunsinger, George O., 119, 122, 127
Hunt, Anne, 116–17
Hurtado, Larry W., 84
Husserl, Edmund, 28

Ignatius Loyola, St., viii, xii, 22, 37, 60, 72, 85, 90–92, 94–97, 107, 140
Imbelli, Robert P., 115, 144
Innocent III, Pope, 67
Iparraguire, Ignacio, 93
Irenaeus, St., 44
Irons, Jeremy, 64
Ivereigh, Austen, 100

James, William, 24
James I, King, 22, 23, 73
Janowiak, Paul A., 134
Jensen, Joseph, 137
Johann, Robert O., 29
John Chrysostom, St., 59
John Paul I, Pope, 130
John Paul II, St., iii, vii, 21, 27, 30, 35–36, 45, 67–68, 124, 143

John XXIII, St., 18, 54–55, 60, 82, 97, 101–2, 106, 108, 115
Jonsen, Albert R., 132
Jossua, Jean Pierre, 143
Jungmann, Josef A., 58, 60, 92, 133–34
Jurgensmeier, Charles, 134
Justin Martyr, St., vii, 22

Kant, Immanuel, 23, 27
Kaplan, Grant, 117
Karekin I, Katholikos, 47
Kaslyn, Robert J., 65, 134
Kasper, Walter, Cardinal, 40, 110
Keating, John R., 86
Keenan, Charles R., 129
Keenan, James F., xi, xiii, 56–57, 99, 116, 117, 133, 143
Kelly, Gerald, ix, xi, 55
Kelly, William J., 107
Kennedy, John Fitzgerald, President, 104
Kennedy, T. Frank, 134
Kilgallen, John J., 87
Kilmartin, Edward J., 43
King, Martin Luther, 63
Kleutgen, Joseph, 12, 128
Klubertanz, George P., 26
Knorn, Bernard, 128
Kolarcik, Michael F., 138
Komonchak, Joseph A., 112, 139, 141, 142, 143
König, Franz, Cardinal, 118
Koning, Robin, xiii
Koterski, Joseph W., xiii, 30, 128
Küng, Hans, 103–4, 142
Kupke, Raymond J., 124
Kurz, William S., 87
Kuzniewski, Anthony, 123, 124–25

LaBelle, Jeffrey, iii
LaFarge, John, xi, 14–15, 54, 90–91, 127
Laffey, Alice L., 136, 137
Lagrange, Marie-Joseph, 74–75
Lainez, Diego, 72
Lapide, Cornelius a, 72, 136
Latourelle, René, 37–39, 111–12, 126, 131
Lattey, Cuthbert, 74
Lauer, Quentin, 28, 120
Laurance, John D., 43
Lawler, Michael G., 99
Ledóchowski, Wlodzimierz, 23
Leontius of Byzantium, 46
Leo XIII, Pope, 4, 9, 12, 14, 23, 53, 71, 75–76, 91
Lera, J. M., 136
Lercher, Ludwig, 12
Liberatore, Matteo, 12
Lienhard, Joseph T., 45–46, 49, 131
Liguori, St. Alphonsus, 53
Lincoln, Abraham, President, 65
Linehan, Dennis M., 142
Livingstone, E. A., 134, 136
Lohfink, Nobert, 83
Loisy, Alfred, 13
Lonergan, Bernard J., x, xi, xiii, 25, 28–31, 37–38, 49, 121, 129, 130
Lord, Daniel A., xi, 14, 54, 62–63, 90–91, 126, 134
Lucas, Thomas M., 133
Luciani, Rafael, 118

Luther, Martin, 110, 115, 145
Lyonnet, Stanislaus, 82

Maas, Anthony J., 73–74, 120, 121, 136
Machuca, A. Vargas, 136
Macken, Theodore, 43, 61
MacKenzie, Roderick A. F., 80–82, 86
MacKinnon, Edward, 32
MacRae, George W., 77–79, 119, 137
Maczkiewicz, Keith, 126, 134, 140
Madges, William, 131
Madigan, Arthur R., 30
Madigan, Daniel A., xiii
Maio, Romeo de, 138
Maldonado, Carlos, 9
Maldonado, Juan, 72, 136
Maloney, George A., 97
Maly, Eugene H., 81
Marcel, Gabriel, 24
Marcus, Joel, 84
Maréchal, Joseph, 27
Maritain, Jacques, x, 23–24, 27–28
Marmion, Declan, 118
Martin, James J., xiii, 85, 95, 131, 137
Martindale, C. C., 74
Martini, Carlo Maria, Cardinal, iii, xi, 78, 85, 91, 137
Martis, John, xiii
Massa, Mark S., 48, 133
Massaro, Thomas J., 66, 134, 135
Mazzella, Cardinal Camillo, xi, 8–9, 75–76, 127
McAuley, Joseph, xiii
McBride, Margaret Mary, 68
McCarthy, Dennis J., 87
McCool, Francis J., 82
McCool, Gerald A., 37, 126
McCormick, Richard A., xi, 56, 133
McDermott, Brian O., 39
McDonough, Peter, 127, 132
McEvoy, James G., 108
McElroy, Robert W., Bishop, 100
McFadden, William C., 9, 124, 125, 126, 128
McGarry, William, 77
McKenzie, John L., 80–81
McKevitt, Gerald, 126
McLuhan, Marshall, 26
McMillen-Evans, Shannon, xiii
McNaspy, C. J., 134
McNicholl, Ambrose, 20
Meconi, David V., 46
Melloni, Alberto, 141, 142
Melville, Annabelle M., 123
Merton, Thomas, x
Mesa, José Alberto, 134
Meszaros, Andrew, 144
Metzger, Bruce M., 78
Michel, Virgil G., 92
Miles, John ("Jack"), 83
Miros, David, xiii
Molina, J. Michelle, 129
Molina, Luis de, 23, 30, 129
Moltmann, Jürgen, 35
Monet, Jacques, 129, 130
Mooney, Christopher F., 35
Moran, William L., 82, 93
Morgenthau, Hans, 63
Moriarty, Frederick L., 77, 80, 86
Morrill, Bruce T., 58–59
Mueller, Joseph G., 108

Muller, William, xiii
Mundelein, George William, Cardinal, viii–ix
Munitiz, Joseph A., 94
Murphy, Francis Xavier, 103
Murphy, G. Roland, 124
Murphy, Roland E., 77, 78, 137
Murphy, Thomas, 123, 126
Murray, John Courtney, xi, 4–5, 15, 18, 54–55, 81–82, 104, 106, 119, 125, 127, 132
Murray, Joyce, 135
Murray, Paul, 140
Mussolini, Benito, 24

Nelson, J. Robert, 108
Neuhaus, Richard J., 63
Newman, St. John Henry, 16, 55, 93
Newton, Sir Isaac, 35
Neyrey, Jerome H., 87
Nickoloff, James B., 135
Niebuhr, Reinhold, 63
Nixon, Richard, President, 66
Noonan, John T., xiii
North, Robert, 77, 82, 139

Oakes, Edward T., ix
Oberman, Heiko, 103
O'Boyle, Patrick, Cardinal, 56
O'Brien, Kevin F., 130
O'Brien, William J., 124
O'Brien, William P., 133
O'Callaghan, Roger T., 79, 138
Ochozor, Paulinus Ikechukwu, 133
O'Connell, Daniel J. K., 121
O'Connell, Gerard, 100
O'Connell, Robert J., 45–46
O'Connor, Roc, 134
O'Donnell, John J., 39
O'Donovan, Leo J., 37, 109, 130
Oesterreicher, John M., 138
O'Hanlon, Daniel J., 18, 103
O'Hara, Edwin V., Archbishop, 77, 137
O'Leary, Brian, 140
O'Malley, John W., xii, 49, 60, 109–10, 112, 114, 116, 118, 120, 132, 141
Onclin, William H, 108
O'Neill, Charles E., 124, 125
Ong, Walter J., x, 25–27, 119–120, 129
Origen, 45, 46
Ormerod, Neil, 49, 113, 132
Orsy, Ladislas, xi, xiii, 42, 65–67, 117, 135
Osiek, Carolyn, 78
O'Toole, Robert F., 139
Ottaviani, Alfredo, Cardinal, 82

Padberg, John W., xiii, 48, 49, 97, 129
Palmer, Paul F., 7, 125
Paris, John J., 57
Parsch, Pius, 92
Passelecq, Georges, 127
Paternostro, David C., 129
Paul III, Pope, 72
Paul VI, St., 18, 56, 101, 105, 119
Pavan, Cardinal Pietro, 54, 106
Pecci, Gioacchino. *See* Leo XIII, Pope
Peck, Gregory, 63
Pecklers, Keith F., 58, 134, 140

Pelikan, Jaroslav, 104
Perčič, Janez, 132
Percy, Walker, x
Perkins, Pheme, 78
Perszyk, Kenneth J., 129
Peters, Ted, 130
Peterson, Daniel, xiii
Phan, Peter C., 116, 117, 135
Philips, Gérard, 138
Photius, Patriarch of Constantinople, 51
Piccirillo, Carlo, 9
Pidel, Aaron, 132–33
Pierce, Joanne M., 133
Pisano, Stephen F., 139
Pius X, St., xi, 12–14, 76, 92
Pius XI, Pope, 15, 91
Pius XII, Pope, 7, 13, 15–16, 45, 75–76, 91–92
Planck, Max, 28
Plantinga, Alvin, 30
Plato, 21
Plowden, Charles, 123
Poché, Justin, 126, 127, 132
Polanyi, Michael, 21
Pope, Stephen J., 130
Provost, James H., 143
Puhl, Louis J., 94

Quasten, Johannes, 120

Rafferty, Oliver P., xiii, 48, 126, 128, 129
Rahner, Karl, viii, x–xi, xiii, 34, 36–37, 60, 64, 102, 106, 109–11, 115, 118, 126, 129, 130, 134, 143
Ramsey, Ian, Bishop, 21
Ramsey, Paul, 108
Ratzinger, Joseph, Cardinal, 68, 106, 110, 115, 135, 142, 144
Rausch, Thomas P., 39
Rees, Martin, 49
Regan, Thomas J., xiii, 30
Rehg, William R., xiii, 30
Richards, John Havens, 10, 18
Richardson, William J. R., 28, 129
Rigaux, Beda, 81
Risk, James E., 65
Robertson, Clare, 133
Romeo, Antonino, 82
Ronayne, Mary John, 132, 138
Roothaan, Jan, 9
Rossiter, Francis S., 137
Rouët de Journel, Marie Joseph, 44
Rourke, Paul K., xiii, 129
Routhier, Giles, 116
Ruether, Rosemary Radford, 69, 135
Ruffini, Ernesto, Cardinal, 41, 117
Rufinus of Aquileia, 47
Ruiz, Gregorio, 136
Rush, Ormond, xiii, 113, 116, 118
Russell, Robert J., 130
Russo, Nicholas, 127
Rynne, Xavier. *See* Murphy, Francis Xavier

Salcedo, Jorge, 134
Saldarini, Anthony ("Tony") J., 83
Salmeron, Alfonso, 72
Salsmans, Joseph, 55
Salzman, Todd A., 99

Sanks, T. Howland, 111, 135, 143
Scannone, Juan Carlos, 98
Scatena, Silvia, 142
Schillebeeckx, Edward, 130
Schindler, David, 132
Schineller, J. Peter, 114, 128, 132
Schloesser, Stephen R., xiii, 49, 109, 117, 128, 132, 143
Schönborn, Christoph, Cardinal, 100
Schrödinger, Erwin, 28
Schroth, Raymond A., 8, 24, 98, 123, 125, 127, 132, 137, 144
Schultenhover, David G., 117, 126, 143
Schutte, Dan, 134
Schweitzer, Albert, 74
Segundo, Juan Luis, 68–69
Semmelroth, Otto, 60, 113, 117
Senior, Donald, 78, 136, 137, 139
Shea, Henry, 129, 140, 141
Shea, John G., 9–10
Sheen, Martin, 64
Sheeran, Michael, xiii
Shenouda III, Pope, 47
Siegman, Edward F., 77
Simone, Michael R., 87
Smith, Brian H., 135
Smith, Simon E., xiii, 139
Smulders, Pieter, 115
Sobrino, Jon, 69, 135
SooHoo, Anthony P., 87
Spadafora, Francesco, 82
Spadaro, Antonio, 99
Spalding, Henry S., 11, 90
Spalding, Thomas W., 123
Spohn, William C., 57–58
Stanley, David M., 77, 85, 91, 104–5, 142
Stegman, Thomas D., 87
Steinmueller, John E., 81
Stoeger, William, 36, 49, 130
Stourton, Charles Philip, 124
Stourton, Edward, 124
Suárez, Francisco, 9, 22–23, 126, 128
Suchecky, Bermond, 127
Sullivan, Francis A., x, 39–43, 49, 56, 90, 102, 109, 112–15, 130, 131
Sweeney, Francis, 103–4
Swetnam, James H., 87, 112
Synge, John, 28

Taft, Robert, 59, 112, 120
Tagle, Luis Antonio G., 142
Taparelli d'Azeglio, Luigi, 12
Tavard, George H., 69, 109
Teilhard de Chardin, Pierre, 35, 98, 109, 143
Teske, Roland J., 45, 46
Tetlow, Joseph A., 128
Theodore of Mopsuestia, 41
Thomson, Geoff, xiii
Thurston, Herbert, 12
Tobin, Thomas H., 87, 139
Toner, Jules J., 95
Toulmin, Stephen, 132
Tracy, David, xii–xiii
Tucci, Roberto, Cardinal, 18
Turing, Alan, 21
Tyrrell, George, 13, 126

Ulrich, Eugene C., 83

Vagnozzi, Egidio, Cardinal, 81
Van Ackeren, Gerald F., ix
Velati, Mauro, 141
Voermans, Sabine, xiii
Vogt, Ernst, 81–82, 138–39
Vollert, Cyril A., ix, 23
Vorgrimler, Herbert, 138, 141

Walsh, James, 94, 98
Ward, Miriam, 78
Waters, Kevin, 134
Weigel, Gustave A., 4–5, 17–18, 40, 49, 90, 104, 107, 127
Whelan, Joseph P., 126
White, Robert A., 112
Whitehead, Alfred North, 26
Wicks, Jared, x, xii, xiii, 39, 48–49, 90, 109–10, 112–13, 115–16, 120, 126, 130, 140, 143, 144
Wiesel, Elie, x
Wild, Robert A., 87
Wilkins, John, 134, 139
Willcock, Christopher, 58, 59, 134
William of Auvergne, 45
Wilson, George B., 108
Wittgenstein, Ludwig, 26
Wood, Susan K., 127, 130
Worcester, Thomas, xv, 48, 134, 140
Wright, George Ernest, 78
Wulf, Friedrich, 94
Wynne, John J., 11

Yarnold, Edward, 58, 59
Young, Erika, 138
Young, Simon, 138

Zabala Lana, Félix, 134
Zerwick, Maximillian ("Max"), 82